Gustavus Adolphus College:
KINGDOM OF IDENTITY

Go around Zion in procession,
Count her towers,
Note her ramparts,
Pass her buildings in review;
That you may tell
The next generation,
That this is God,
Our God from eternity.
He shall be our guide.

Psalm 48:12-14

For Stephanie Christine

Born November 28, 1966

The night was clear,
And cold as apple's skin.
Orion was climbing the valley stair,
When you came.

O be beautiful as Helen, your mother,
Holy as Mary!
And may the kind God let you go
Dancing through the autumn glow.

Gustavus Adolphus College:
KINGDOM OF IDENTITY

by Richard Quentin Elvee

with illustrations by Michael Bennes

ILLUSTRATIONS

Autumn 15

Butterfly 19

Transfiguration 33

Greed 39

Tree 63

An Old Friend 71

Doorway in Time 99

Copernicus and Cross 113

Sonata Baccalaureus 133

Summer's Evening 139

CONTENTS

Acknowledgments..9

Introduction..11

Kingdom of Identity...12

September Beginnings..14

Opening Convocation...17

When You Are Young You See Things Separately......................18

There Is Something About the Church...............................21

My Father Died in September.......................................22

Freshman Sunday...25

Crossing the Bar..28

The First Sunday After a Football Loss............................30

And Signs to Us From the Past Are the Language of God.............35

Parents Day...36

Day of the Visiting Academic Deans................................38

Cry the Beautiful Boys..42

Burning the Weeds: All Flesh is Grass.............................43

The Old Peace of God..44

Requiem for a Coach...46

Luther and His Mom..51

Luther and His Dog..53

Thrice Hail, Gus..55

November 22, 1963...56

Beard...57

Examination Before Christmas Vacation.............................61

Adventus Domini...62

Now the Animals Go to Sleep.......................................67

Sermon for the Aud..70

Free for Nothing or Free for Something?...........................73

February..77

Transfiguration...79

Spring Light..85

Good Friday...87

God's Body..88

Other Voices, Other Rooms...90

Fridays After the Resurrection....................................95

A Doorway in Time...98

The Good Shepherd..102

Tony Crawford..103

End of the Vietnam War...104

Joseph Nicolas Nicollet..107

Spring Sermon..111

St. Copernicus...112

Sermon for the End of a Term.....................................116

Pentecost: Festival of the Holy Spirit...........................118

The Prodigal Son...121

Mellow 1975..123

Tell Them That They Were Good....................................125

Trinity Sunday...129

Sonata Baccalaureus..132

Summer Altar...137

ACKNOWLEDGMENTS

This book is a letter to my mother, Nelle Vandenberg,
to my Michigan aunts, Mabel and Florence,
to my sisters, Marianne, Janice and Phyllis.

It is also for Stephen Eckman and Paul Strandness:
     students, cherished friends, generous patrons of this book;
for Edgar Carlson who opened the door to it;
for Jack Clark and William Dean who created theological space for it;
for Lawrence Owen and the Uncalled, who called for it;
for Robert Peterson and Kelvin Miller who believed in it, and were indispensable;
for Jeanie who collected it, Janine who typed it, Linda who lived with it,
and John Rezmerski who fixed it;
for Kathryn and Elaine who assisted it,
and for Michael Bennes who saw it right away.

It is also for Esby who wrote letters when I was weak,
and for Ruth who was there every day, and wrote the Introduction.

It is for my colleagues who cared along the way,
and for the Golden Gusties and their parents, who listened with love.

Finally, it is to Geoffrey, whom I watch with pride.

Richard Q. Elvee

Grateful acknowledgment is made to the following for permission to reprint previously published material:

Fortress Press, Philadelphia, for "When You Are Young You See Things Separately," Renewal in the Pulpit: Sermons by Young Preachers, ed. by Edmund A. Steimle, 1966. Incorporated in this selection are lines of poetry by Li Po, translated by Witter Bynner, from The Wisdom of China and India, ed. Lin Yutang, Modern Library, 1955.

Acknowledgment is made of the following sources of quoted material:

Jurgen Habermas, "Hans-Georg Gadamer," in Philosophical-Political Profiles, the MIT Press, 1983.

Robert Frost, "October," Complete Poems of Robert Frost, Holt, Rinehart, and Winston, 1964.

Theodore Roethke, "Transplanting," The Collected Poems, Doubleday and Company, 1966.

Karl Barth, "Kant," <u>Protestant Thought: From Rousseau to Ritschl</u>, Harper and Brothers, 1959.

Dietrich Bonhoeffer, "Christians and Pagans," in <u>Letters and Papers from Prison</u>, translated by Christian Kaiser Verlag, Macmillan Publishing Company, Inc., 1972.

T.S. Eliot, "Journey of the Magi" and "Little Gidding," <u>The Complete Poems and Plays</u>, Harcourt, Brace and Company, 1958.

Dylan Thomas, "The Force That Through the Green Fuse," <u>The Collected Poems of Dylan Thomas</u>, New Directions, 1953.

Jorge Luis Borges, "Paradiso XXXI, 108," <u>A Personal Anthology</u>, Grove Press, 1967.

Gustaf Wingren, Prayers, in <u>The Christian View of Faith and Life</u>, translated by Edgar M. Carlson, Augsburg Publishing, 1981.

Gustavus Adolphus College gratefully acknowledges a 125th anniversary gift from Aid Association for Lutherans which has helped to make possible the publication of this book of sermons.

INTRODUCTION

Can a sermon be a work of art?

When van Gogh took paint and brush to a canvas, bright orange, greens and yellows became a scene.

When Bach put little black notes on paper, we heard music never heard before.

When Granlund molded clay into human form, new concepts of shape made sense.

When Gustavus Chaplain Richard Q. Elvee preaches a sermon, it is done with that kind of creativity. He makes words sing, and paint, and dance. His words can evoke feelings of tenderness, nostalgia, laughter, sorrow, despair, skepticism, hope—and most of all transcendence.

His sermons are created out of his own perception of nature, literature, philosophy, great women and men (new pictures of Luther keep emerging!), and the Word which is nearly always present in new understanding.

He is a great reader of books of every kind that are the background for his own creative thought. He frequently quotes favorite passages, blending them into his own phrases, just as he is able to articulate the Lutheran faith in such a way as to make it contemporary.

For many years Richard Elvee has been asked to have some of his sermons published, but he has said that a sermon, like the closing argument of a lawyer, is to be heard, not read. However, those of us who have listened to him on tape often find the sermons as fresh as when he preached them.

Now Chaplain Elvee has agreed, for the 125th anniversary of Gustavus, which is also the twenty-fifth anniversary of his ministry in Christ Chapel, to gather together a selection of his sermons into a volume that can be read.

Through the sermons in this book, others may share in the experience of worshipping in Christ Chapel, the chapel that for many is the heart of Gustavus where the life of the Spirit is kept alive in academia.

—Ruth Esbjornson
Gustavus Adolphus College
Bernadotte Library Staff, 1963-83

KINGDOM OF IDENTITY

O it is time to go . . . I know . . . Gustavus?
Gustavus has been a home to you for four years.
You do not realize, in your haste to go just now,
That you are leaving a home. That you will come back
To this home, all your life.
Gustavus is a special kind of home, a mystical home.
You leave it today; still, you never really leave,
No matter where in this world you go.
All your life you will stay in it.
It appeared to you in your youth;
You will see it when you are old.
It is a Kingdom of Identity—keeper of dreams, expectations!

What was it you sought in this house? What vision?
What fair, gracious, beautiful thing did you dream?
The meaning of life? The conscience of history?
Blessedness? The kingdom of light and of God?
O Journey! O Faust! O Lord Jesus!
O golden ground of music!
O shining world of nature!
O GUSTAVUS!

SEPTEMBER

SEPTEMBER BEGINNINGS

Lord it is time...the summer was too long.

—Rainer Maria Rilke

After you are here a few Septembers, you will learn for yourself that the life of this little college is imprinted by the natural world in which it is set. Fall beginnings, middle-winter marches, late spring endings. And then once more, again, once more.

September beginnings! All the young blood hawks flown back from summer. All the countryside gone amber. All the skies gone blue, cerulean blue, Mediterranean blue. All the squirrels gone nuts! All the frogs gone crazy, humming, drumming, booming, croaking. All the campus nights gone gardens of Spain!

I hope you will like this place. It's a good place to grow in. Grow up tall! Grow out of a narrow, selfish uncertain childhood, becoming a large, competent, tender Beast, O God, Kant and Thomas Wolfe! After you are here a few Septembers!

Autumn

14

OPENING CONVOCATION

Mes chers collegues et amis!

Sure and what rivals the splendor of this September morning! The academic colors of this tribal gathering on a late summer campus. It is a golden light that shines on this little college world, on the undergraduate years; a frail beautiful light, soon enough withdrawing into the world's shadowed places. So taste these years! They quickly pass! Even if this is your twentieth go-round, you will lose happiness and strength if you do not feel the exhilaration of this day, of this season and this place.

This is our spring time. There is in it expectation and experiment, new hope and new circumstance. There is an instinct which tells us we should grasp this day. For although our life is meant for continuity, it is no less meant for new starts. Here is strength waiting for work. The two are just upon the point of meeting. Everything shines with vigor and hope. There is no limit to the work which we dream may be done before the season is over.

Assuredly, it was a rotten summer! Too brief, too wet, too insect-infested to have offered any relief from the duress of the last academic year. But let all of that go. Here is a new beginning. Our great house is open again. The lights are on in all the rooms. And the sons and daughters of Adam and Christ hurry through the campus twilights! Godspeed!

WHEN YOU ARE YOUNG YOU SEE THINGS SEPARATELY

When you are young you see things separately.
Yesterday in the science hall
I saw the butterfly
transfixed on a pin.
And I thought of all the butterflies
in the dusty halls of colleges,
sitting erect in cabinets of glass,
spoils of the scientist
who netted their brief flight,
pinned their thin thread breath on wood,
stamped them with his words—
nymphalidae, hesperidae, metazoa, insecta—
caught and classified,
stored away in a little corner of knowledge.

When you are young, you see things
    separately.
Nature stands alone, apart.
After a while, things join together.
You fall into nature, nature into you.

You are the secret of the butterfly,
The butterfly is the secret of you.
You become a world.

You become a world—
September afternoon of another year,
the butterfly, still yellow with August,
raced behind Old Main,
and you chased the thing—wing, and dance.

You become a world, sad, mortal.
Like the butterfly,
you were caught that sunny afternoon
by death, you, Gustie, O you!
Replaced by others
who walk the campus in the October light.

You become a world, lonely, longing.
Before the door, where you went away,
each footprint is overgrown with green moss
so deep that none can sweep it away.

The first autumn wind added the falling leaves.
And now in September, yellowing butterflies
hover two by two in our west garden grasses.
And because of all this, my heart is breaking
and I fear for my bright cheeks lest they fade.

Mornings like this in late summer, when I sit
    in the Chapel, waiting
for the service to begin, sometimes the
    butterfly will flutter along
outside the Chapel glass, like a piece of
    paper in the wind. And I wonder
how such little things in the world should
    move
beside the big, an insect beside a temple.

They belong together!

O brought us the colors of paradise!
Tulip's fire, sheen of cherry blossom,
Canvases of yellow suns that set in Eden.
O brought us the world we lost,
going into exile!
When we filled the earth, they multiplied in
    the hedge.
They spread and spread over the plains.

The night the ovens were lit
at Auschwitz,
they slept in the tall autumn grasses.
All of the long summer after Jesus died,
they struggled out of cocoons
in the soft morning light.

When you are young you see things separately.
After a while, you see them together.
You become a world.
You are...god...in God.

Butterfly

THERE IS SOMETHING ABOUT THE CHURCH

There is something about the Church
that is like the wind that flows through the campus fields
on autumn days: constant, ancient and mysterious.
Most of you have missed this Something thus far.
There are no continuities in your life.
You are deaf to ancient words.
You have no sense at all of the inside of things.
Your life is one glossy externality, and it stinks!
You cannot say: *I live in mystery.*
I know.

And there comes a time when you find
the bread and wine
of the Church insipid.
You look elsewhere for nourishment.
The bread and wine of the inns, which you find on the highways,
at the crossroads, alone can appease your hunger and thirst.
And the inns are a heck-of-a-lot more interesting and exciting.
I know.
But, you cannot spend all of your life in inns.
There is something about the Church.
I know.

MY FATHER DIED IN SEPTEMBER

We come here today to mourn the death of our beloved husband and father. We the children come to raise this tribute to our father. He was a father to so many people, that this picture we present is necessarily partial and incomplete, these words but a little island in the great sea of unspoken memories he left in that great number of people whose lives he touched. Nor is there world enough, or time, to say all that is in our hearts. So each of us is left in the quiet of this hour with private memories which we may say only to God.

He touched all of us, and he lives on in all of us, but we the children had a special relationship to him. We were flesh to his flesh, bone to his bone; he and our mother gave us life. So we must raise up as with hands of thanksgiving the days of our years—springtime and harvest, winter and summer, water and music and stars. The voices that rise out of a golden childhood—our father's certain whistle over the quiet waters of green-gold afternoons of play. And home we went to large rambling parsonages, where there were laughter and tears and the festive board. Often, they were shelter for the stranger passing in the street. We remember the jack-o-lantern in the window at Halloween; the snow that fell and fell in the backyard at Christmas; and most of all, our father's voice. These things we must raise up now, these things raise as with hands of thanksgiving to bless the memory of our father and the God of every good and perfect gift.

He was a great and good man, vital, alive, aware. A man at home in his times, for he loved the busy life of the great American cities. This was always his church—the city, the whole city. From the time when he wandered the Depression streets of Chicago as a young Moody student, until his last days on the freeways of Los Angeles, the noisy, bustling excitement of the city was his life, the patient murmuring voices of its multitudes, the din of office and factory and great ships at sea, the sweat of ten thousand laboring hands in Chicago and Buffalo and Gary and Minneapolis. He was at home in a train depot, a bus station, an airport, at home among the strangers who milled there. Their life—the common life of people, of buying and selling in the market place, of departing from and returning to loved ones—was his life; he loved it.

And all people were his equals; he was democratic to the core. For him everyone had dignity. "No man is an island," said the old English preacher Donne; to Father, no one was a stranger. He reverenced something in them all, even the most petty and weak and vicious among them. And they found him too. They sought him out. People in trouble, total strangers who, drifting out to sea, could pick him out of a hotel lobby. They found him like moths find a street light on a dark night. And mostly, mostly he was able to help them, the stranger and the friend alike. He was a master counselor, to those high and low. He was a superb listener. He made folk over again. He made them endure. He gave them a new lease on life. He was to them, a great harbor. He led them home.

Of course he would not have said this of himself. He would have said it was of God, though he did not speak easily of God. He always retained something of that austere awesome feeling which his people, the Holland people, felt in the presence of the Eternal Majesty. He did not speak easily of God. But he readily spoke of the kindly Jesus, the Saviour. "The Lord," he would say, "the Lord." For this was the supreme overarching experience of his life. This is what wrenched him out of his own country and away from his own beloved people, to become a wanderer in the earth, a man for all men. As surely as the ancient apostle was visited on the road to Damascus, in June 1930 a young salesman, traveling on the road to sell in some great city, was laid upon and stamped with the marks of the Eternal, and those marks were Christ, and he was marked for life. For that experience and that experience alone he gave up what might have been a large share in the riches of this world. This was the root out of which the branches of his life flourished.

At midday, O king, I saw a light from heaven, and I said, Who art thou, Lord? And he said, I am Jesus whom thou persecutest. But rise, and stand upon your feet: For I have appeared unto you for this purpose, to make you a minister and a witness to the Gentiles, unto whom now I send you, to open their eyes, and to turn them from darkness to light, and from the power of Satan unto God, that they may receive forgiveness of sins, and inheritance among those who are sanctified by faith that is in me. Whereupon, O King Agrippa, I was not disobedient unto the heavenly vision.

This was our father. These words describe him. This is what people heard from him in city streets, in temples along those city streets. We can still hear his voice above the din of the cities, calling, calling men to this Jesus of Nazareth. *Whereupon, O King Agrippa, I was not disobedient unto the heavenly vision.* Ah, this was our father.

But quickly now, we must mention his interest in a people peculiarly related to the life and growth of American cities, the Jewish people. In them he had a deep and abiding interest. Perhaps it was out of his childhood, the Hebrew psalms which the Holland people revered; the special feeling they had of being themselves the children of Abraham; the awe and mystery which for them surrounded the name of Jehovah. Whatever the source, always, everywhere, from the beginning of his ministry to the end, Father felt he was one of them. Whatever the origin, he seemed to understand them; businessman and rabbi, he understood them at some level where the water of life runs deep. Sometimes on Friday night he wore the little black cap and preached down at the synagogue, and they called him "Rabbi." And he was a rabbi, a teacher. For he was an educated man. Against superior odds, graduating from high school at twenty-four with wife and children to support, he pursued learning which eventually led him to the highest degrees from the most learned institutions in America. Nor was this a fruitless education, an empty venture. For he became a teacher of teachers, a leader among leaders. To the great religious and social issues of his time he was intensely alive, and always he prodded and pushed his colleagues and people out of their parochialisms, their futile attempts to achieve identity by gathering in small and illiberal groups. He was always enlarging their horizons. Something there was in him that didn't love a wall. And he led them into larger paths than those to which they were accustomed. He pushed them out into the broad stream of humanity, and showed them that they'd never know the fullness of the glory of God in their little windowless boxes, for it flowed through the interstices of the world everywhere, for it was as large as the earth and all its people.

Marianne, our sister, last night thought of the words of Thoreau, and they seem right to describe him, for Father was a supreme practitioner of this art. *The art of awareness,* wrote Thoreau, *is the act of learning how to wake up to the external miracle of life with limitless possibilities.* He was always expectant, Father. He saw the flame of life in the most unexpected places and people, and rejoicing to see it, he cupped it in his hands and blew upon it, and it would grow larger and brighter, and he would be glad.

Finally, before we close, we must speak briefly for our mother. Father was not like those men who, golden in the public eye, had feet of clay at home. She had from him in larger measure the same understanding, compassion and love he gave to all people. Our feelings about her on this day are strong and silent and deep. Let us say simply that our father received from her the supreme and singular gift of life. He'd not have been much to others without her. She was his life.

And of so much else we have not time to speak now: of his bright humor and goodness, of his work and recreation, of his aspirations and worship. Now, too, we must carry him back across the mountains and plains of this great country he loved, to the state of his birth, Michigan. Where the autumn mists rise in the chill air of an advancing year. Where along the roadsides he knew so well, the spikes of goldenrod and purple aster have replaced the white and yellow clovers of summer. Where a fire is lit in the scarlet of the maples and the ducks gather in the dusk of ponds. Where the great oaks in the yards of Grand Rapids have begun to drop their acorns one by one, as a midwestern year ripens to another harvest. It is also Father's harvest. *For the silver cord is loosed, the golden bowl is broken. The pitcher is broken at the fountain, and the wheel is broken at the cistern. The dust must return to the earth as it was, and the spirit unto God who gave it.*

And we, the family, pray that in the quiet of this hour, you who knew him and loved him last, will become one with us in the resolve to carry on for ourselves, for our families, and for all people of the world, his life of compassion and the reconciliation of all to each other and to their God.

Richard A. Elvee, President of Northwestern College, St. Paul, Minnesota, from 1952 to 1957, died in September, 1968.

FRESHMAN SUNDAY

Thou art a mere freshie . . .

Dear lowly freshmen, brothers and sisters, and others. Freshman Sunday at Gustavus has something about it very much its own. This is the first unhurried morning, after all sorts of busyness and anxiety in getting located on this hill. Even the campus, accustomed as it is to the student parade, for which it furnishes so fine a setting, welcomes a Sunday's quiet. The chimes of the chapel have a lovelier music today. For a few hours the competing voices are silenced. So they begin to weave the magic web, half of melody, half of memory, which will become the music of our lives. The bells will call to you, again and again from this church at the center. And when the time comes that you cannot come at their call, you will hear the bells in your dreams. This Christhouse always opens its doors expectantly. It has become by its own right, the center upon which many paths converge. It knows its secure place in the life of this college; its indispensable service to the human spirit. It knows how to open its doors. It knows how to wait.

For many of you, this morning is the fulfillment of many dreams and hopes. Here in the friendly company of your peers, you realize for the first time, that your college life has begun. You begin to sense that you belong. You are a member in good standing of a good college! It is a milestone in your life—of which there are, after all, not so many. There is a moving passage in *David Copperfield*, where David with Agnes by his side looks through a window into the winter twilight, and sees in retrospect, the long road by which he has come to happiness. Some such road we always see in our moments of high realization. I think it some such road that I traveled last night in my reveries, so that I couldn't sleep, the road along which many years ago I went to college.

I didn't sleep much last night, thinking about you over in the residence halls, perhaps awake too, listening to the late summer insects in their noisy conversation. On the college lawns, in the surrounding fields, they talked all night of love, of territory, of the moon in its last quarter, of life and expectation, and just the gentle urge to go on, to make it! Perhaps you were awake too, listening to the voices, wondering about the future, reflecting on that great speech of Professor Owen at the Freshman banquet, on getting into the Conversation. It kept me awake too, wondering what I might add to it on a quiet Sunday morning.

You might begin by communicating with that insect mind out in the campus grass! What were they talking about all night? Sexual arousal? Certainly that! You might ask them about it. You might learn from them that they don't just mate with any cricket coming through the grass! They are very discriminating! They are not only concerned about having sex. They are interested in something beyond sex: the quality of the species! What else were they talking about? About territory! There is your space, this is my space. You put your clothes over there and keep your mate over there, too. They talked about the weather. This is Minnesota! You can tell how hot it is by how fast they talk.

O September! O the freshman heart!

OCTOBER

CROSSING THE BAR

Sunset and evening star,
And one clear call for me!
And may there be no moaning of the bar,
When I put out to sea.

John was a meek man. John Chindvall was a gentle person, the sort we had hoped would inherit the earth. John's gentleness was a gift to him from his parents who are gentle people. John was also very smart. In this time when intelligence and technical reason are preeminent qualifications for success, he was better equipped than most of us to succeed. And he had many plans and ideas he wished to pursue. He would have made his way in the world very well.

It appeared to us, also, that behind John's wry smile was an adult maturity, newly achieved—a knowledge of the world and its ways, which made him more certain than before. Now, he could get on with it. He could spread his wings to fly. The preparation was long, mostly invisible, but the young tree could now bring forth its leaf in its season. Then, sudden, as the arrow that flies at noon, sudden, as the storm that roots up a tree, he was down, he was gone.

But such a tide as moving seems asleep,
Too full for sound and foam,
When that which drew from out the boundless deep
Turns again home.

We buried him yesterday in Minneapolis. We cried. We looked around us at the ripening year. We touched our bodies. We sensed that we were hearing and touching and smelling a fresh full day, but that the taste and feel of it had altered. Driving through the comfortable suburbs in the car on the way back to school, we saw the leaves of another year, fallen down in the yards. Some of us knew we must change our lives, make them simpler, purer, truer.

Twilight and evening bell,
And after that the dark!
And may there be no sadness of farewell,
When I embark.

And John, whom we left behind. Whither John? In the 20th century, we don't agree on that. Each is consoled by an interior dream. I do not know what John's was. So I will offer my own reverie on last week's events. John's little car moves along a valley road in a chiaroscuro of autumn, when the picture is torn. There is a blur in the tear; then silence and space, and then a vast water, a great sea.

28

For though from out our bourne of Time and Place
The flood may bear me far,
I hope to see my Pilot face to face
When I have crost the bar.

"I want to see the tropical sea swell," Bob Jackson wrote last June, before he took his own life, "I want to smell the warm salt air, rushing at me from far, far away." In my reverie, there is a harbor on the other side of the sea. One comes to it in the noiseless morning, comes to a beach and fishing boats. Someone is turning fish on the coals of a fire. Someone is passing bread. Safe journey, John! We love you!

John Chindvall '70, Onamia, Minnesota, died October 3, 1970.

Bob Jackson '70, LeSueur, Minnesota, died June 29, 1970.

"Crossing the Bar," Alfred Lord Tennyson

THE FIRST SUNDAY AFTER A FOOTBALL LOSS

I have been crucified with Christ; it is no longer I who live, but Christ who lives in me; and the life I now live in the flesh I live by faith in the Son of God, who loved me and gave himself for me.

—Galatians 2:20

Brothers and sisters, there is an alumnus with us this morning, who always comes to this service on Sunday, after the Gusties have been routed on Saturday at football. I always imagine that he wants an explanation! Or better, he wants that I should demythologize the agonizing loss so that he can live with it! We are like two old crows feasting on road kills. It was a long afternoon yesterday after the Tommies went up by 35 points.

"Coach," I said, "this is a long afternoon."

He said, "There will be more!"

After the game, I pitied myself. I said to my wife: "I want to be the Chaplain of a jock school." Later in the day I met a professor who said, "Chaplain, if you can't do any better than 56 points against, turn the praying over to someone else." Then I knew the defeat was mine also. I settled into one of the early evening Saturdays, trying without benefit of alcohol, to absorb the defeat as best I could. The rest of you went out to play.

The first thing I did was to open my eyes and look around me. I had been squinting for three hours. When I opened my eyes, I saw the valley hills aflame in reds and golds and russets. I saw an orange moon sailing above the autumn tapestry and I saw that I was going to be all right!

In football too you learn how to go down, to enter into defeat in order to suck dry its power to destroy future possibilities. My alumnus friend has learned this off the field; he has overcome a handicap. I love him very much. I hope you, dear frosh, will learn this too, whether you play football or not. Perhaps you will learn it after you are defeated in a friendship, or a test, or when that first paper comes back from Jack Clark, all marked up, and marked down!

There is a word we use out there on the field which seems offensive in church. But I just said it: suck! It is surely a word against the neighbor when used in the old Gustie yell: "Augsburg sucks!" Better we should say, "Augsburg inhales!" But we don't use it that way out there. We say that word to ourselves, or to someone we like who has made a mistake in a game, or who has things going against him. We say to him "Suck it up, friend, suck it up."

"Is there a scripture text for this Sunday, Elvee?"

"I live, yet not I, but Christ lives in me." That is the text. So dear friend alumnus, since you are here, let us turn from football to the Gospel. We haven't stopped losing the big ones, but we haven't changed our theology either! The word you heard years ago when you were a student, you may still hear: that you should always be ready to know that for

Transfiguration

30

which you could be responsible, and become responsible for it! And that in coming to know that responsibility, you should come to know God.

Now froshers, you will hear all year about responsibility. The upperclassmen can tell you that! This morning I wish to speak about knowing God.

Suppose that we really do want to have a relationship with God. That is an enormous supposition, but I don't doubt that you have it when you come here. Most of you come to church for that reason. You seek God. Although the knowledge of God is not only the last, but also the sweetest of things, it can sometimes seem so difficult to come by. We are so in love with our own ideas, plans and habits, that even if falling in with God's plan is pure and deep joy, we do not fall into it with ease. What is the difficulty here? How is it we don't know God very well?

Doubtless God is infinitely active everywhere and in an infinity of spaces. He besets us on every hand. To ask, "What is God doing about us?" is like asking, "What is nature up to?" Imagine stopping with me on Eckman Mall last night: the leaves scattered everywhere; the silent perfuming of the air from the flowers under Christ's bronze body; the sound of many living things in the grass; the complex web of life; and the sense that although this is the natural world, it is at the same time given and a gift. This would be knowledge of God. The action of God is infinite in every finite organism in the world about us. It greets us everywhere. It affects us. It molds us. It is us.

A certain faith gives us the strength to live in this nature, not because it is sustained by miraculous interventions, as if God were to give us a special sign as we crossed the campus at night. Rather, it is as if one and the same occurrence makes us feel that we may in principle understand its natural causes, and at the same time appears to us as supernatural, as an act of God which we receive from him. The action of God is everywhere in the world around us, molds us in every event, calls to us. It is always the next event.

Now in this process, God is at once different from us and identical with us. God is that which confronts us in nature, in the nature which meets us as world in every moment of our existence. So I think of God as outside me, as surrounding me, as confronting me, as creating my natural destiny. In that destiny he gives me both good and evil, joy and sorrow, and I complain to him, I call to him. I try to speak rightly to him as to another person.

But God is also identical with us. This is a Christian idea, that God has become human, and the human has become God. Identity with God frightens us at first. Could this life we are living be the very life of God? What was St. Paul indicating when he said, "I live, or rather not I, but Christ lives in me, and for me to live is Christ"? If we say we cannot understand such language, the difficulty is not about the sense of the words. They are plain enough. The difficulty is one of imagining how we live the life of God.

Just now, I was speaking with you about God as though he were another person who confronts you in nature, who approaches you as your environment. Now I am saying that you who do the confronting and calling in nature are also the life of God. Here we are, making our approach to God, and we are much burdened with our failures, much darkened in our understanding, so that the God of destiny and nature seems quite hidden. Then we remember that God has identified himself with us in our Christic life, so that even our darkness is a kind of divine darkness, is Christ's dark Gethsemane and Calvary; and our prayer is Christ's prayer; and our yearning, Christ's yearning; and our feeble resolves are carried on the tide of his sacrificial will. Eventually, our death is his death.

In the early hours of last Sunday morning, they carried the dead body of the freshman student Barry Armstrong down to the local hospital—out of the sad, autumn-haunted, party evening of freshman welcome, into the antiseptic emergency room. They laid it out, still warm, but dead. After his parents had gone home at three or four a.m., just before turning back to this hill, I went into the emergency room, under the harsh lights, all the engines of medical progress whirring about me, helpless now to put him on any life pathway. Laid out on the table he looked like one of the old paintings of Christ after he had been taken down from the cross and laid out on a slab—quiet, dead.

I walked to the table and touched the body.

Later that morning, I sat in the service at this church. The vicar was preaching on the gospel for the day, in which Christ asks the disciples, "Who do men say that I am?" That is what the body downtown said to me. "Who do men say that I am?" Who are you, Barry? You are a dead freshman, about to become a college statistic. "Is that what you say, Chaplain?"

No, Barry, my brother, growing cold now—even in death, you are the Christ!

Now, if this identity were real to you, Gustie, do you think it would make a difference? If you could say, "For me to suffer is Christ, for me to try to pray is Christ, for me to die is Christ," would that make a difference?

However, suppose you must say, "I can't see things that way. I can't feel things that way." Is that the end of the matter for you? I don't think it need be that, if you are willing to open yourself to the fellowship in this place. In this fellowship Christ comes among us to be our life. When we eat and drink together in his name, his life begins to fill us.

When you were children, sometimes people warned you about being too familiar with the Holy Communion, and it may be true that for children, a certain familiarity with the chancel may breed contempt for what is happening. But it is certainly not that way for us. A familiarity with the life of Christ that is given to us when we gather at this table is exactly what we need. In this sacrament of this presence, he becomes part of the theme and rhythm of our life, and we begin to know that we share his divine life and his divine death in the world. This was how Christ's first disciples also received him, in the breaking of the bread. Many years of such practice lay behind St. Paul when he wrote, "For me to live is Christ." This sacrament is for you if you are sincerely ready, so far as in you lies, to let Christ take you and offer you and your purposes with his own to the God who is your destiny in the world of nature and history unfolding during the days ahead. Come now, let us break bread together on our knees.

Barry Armstrong, a freshman student from White Bear Lake, died September 15, 1982.

AND SIGNS TO US FROM THE PAST ARE
THE LANGUAGE OF GOD

He renders an account of being as tradition, because he does not deliver himself up to the shapeless undertow of an ethereal being, but, casting his gaze back to Hegel, takes into account the massive stream of the tradition of words that have become ob-jective and concrete, actually spoken in their place at their time.

—Habermas on Gadamer

I heard the *Moonlight Sonata* of Beethoven Sunday night last, at that hour of St. Peter twilight when melancholy sets in. It was a moment of quiet beauty. It is gone now. The night in which I heard it is gone. They will not return. All things have rushed on.

But I remember the music, the night! I hope it is not forever gone as it seems, for then it was in fact nothing. I hope it was something. I hope it was a part of something toward which life is moving.

That is what hope must be like, it seems to me. To hold up with hands of thanksgiving the moments that have been, the days that have been, and all the voices that have talked in them. To understand that all the works and words which have disappeared into the silence and darkness behind us were, after all, the real meaning of our being here.

What was it someone said?
The voice of the instructor in the damp autumn room.
The voice of Moses at Sinai.
The voice of David at Jerusalem.
The voice of Socrates in Athens.
What was it someone said?
Gregory at Rome,
Luther at Worms,
Hamilton at Philadelphia.
Lincoln at Gettysburg.
Wilson at Geneva.
Faulkner at Stockholm.
Sandburg at Thanksgiving.

So what are they against the silence? *Nothing!*
So where are those high moments of culture now? *Nowhere!*
They are gone.

But we may love them for having been here. I inscribe today, over the invisible entrance of your education in this college, the injunction, *to love the past*. And I remind you that unless you learn to love, the texts and melodies will finally mean nothing at all. Unless you entertain, earnestly, lovingly, the voices, you will never truly live in history. Unless you bear witness that you belong to all that has been said, you will not become humane.

Finally, to love the past, words and things, is to love God. And to love God, from whom all things proceed and to whom all things return, is to receive everything back from the nothing into which it has disappeared—a dialogue of Plato, a letter of Paul, a melody of Beethoven, the leaves that hurry through this old October day.

PARENTS DAY

There was a rich man, who was clothed in purple and fine linen and who feasted sump-tuously every day. And at his gate lay a poor man named Lazarus, full of sores, who desired to be fed with what fell from the rich man's table.

—Luke 16:19

Slow, slow, you sweetness of October's mild mornings. Old black and gold moving up and down the Ole field just yesterday, bringing home the pumpkin! Another Eppie roast at the farm, and Kappa bust at the barn. Food and wine, and somebody close in the sun and then the dark at Seven Mile—slow now, slow. It was quiet last night over at the library. The Dipper sparkled in the chapel yard, quiet, lonely, deep. The ivy on Old Main was red already—slow, but slow, October; I want to touch you before you go. The river valley too, coming down to see the children grow up: slow, so that we may love you before you go.

The text, Elvee! Oh yes, always the text. The rich man and the beggar for Parents Day. The colored leaves drifting down in the rich man's garden in South Minneapolis, or hurrying after one another down on Hennepin where the beggar shivers, awaiting his particular crumb before winter. It's a poor text for Parents Day, anyway. Who, after all, is the beggar? Do the parents always have to play the rich man?

The parents may be beggars, sitting at the gate of some rich corporation, eating crumbs, waiting to be seen from the big house, brought in to the feast. The parents imagine that they are seen by this college as rich folk, dressed in expensive clothes, driving luxury cars, who are about to be hit up for a few more scraps for the beggar college at the Edina gate! The confusion is compounded by the very disturbing picture of Gustavus nestled in Father Abraham's bosom, and the well-heeled parents and alums who paid it little attention in their lifetime, burning in the flames of hell!

No, it really doesn't work. Doesn't wing you.

There was also a poor man named Lazarus covered with sores, who used to be brought to the rich man's door. I remember reading how it pained the educated aesthete Goethe to look at sick people, the mentally ill. It spoiled his ideal universe. How different, Jesus, who told this parable about this sick man.

You see how it is. In our desire for security and beauty, for some insulation from the world's cares and ills, on a hushed October morning in a private college garden, we may not even see the sick and lame out at the gate at all! There has finally come to be only the luxury of our lives. We are smothered in our perfumes, trapped in the birdlime of our own nest. I'm not somebody back from the dead telling you this, but I am calling out to you this morning: O rich men, O rich ladies! Have you looked out your golden autumn window to see whether a Lazarus is at the gate?

I know how it is. I live in a fine house. I know how success has a way of insulating you behind glass. You didn't imagine when you were here as a student that you could ever become insensitive that way, so removed from human concerns.

But it's easy. Crunching all those numbers down at the office—friend, you dare not become what they would make of you if they could. They provide for you a rich place in the sun, but make it well nigh impossible to see your neighbor in the dark. You can read all the numbers without ever a thought as to what they mean for life, for lifting the burden of things from those least able to carry them.

O hushed October morning mild, thy leaves have ripened to the fall.

You gather us again in the Father's house, the festal table. You gather us parent and child. You make us brothers and sisters in the kingdom of humanity. How strange and new this is! My father, a brother in the kingdom of humanity and responsibility. My mother, a sister in the kingdom of grace, of hopefulness and charity. *Amen.*

DAY OF THE VISITING ACADEMIC DEANS

Then the Lord said to Cain, "Where is Abel your brother?" He said, "I do not know; am I my brother's keeper?"

—Genesis 4:10

"What do you mean by crushing my people, by grinding the face of the poor?" says the Lord God of hosts.

—Isaiah 3:15

Listen, you who grind the poor, who say "When will Fall Break be over, so we may sell corn? When will Sunday be over, so we may sell wheat?" giving short measure in the bushel, doubling the price, so that you can buy a poor man's land for a pair of shoes: "I will not forget what you are doing," says the Lord.

One of the particular advantages to preaching in this college chapel is not to have to preach to the same old crowd every Sunday. There is this propitious turnover of patrons! In the parish church, the patrons turn over the pastor. In the college the pastor turns over the parishioners. Each tranquil autumn delivering carloads of freckled freshmen who love chapel; each foggy, soggy May commencement hauling away the cynical world-weary senior inactives. In between, a smoky October weekend blowing in a whole planeload of somebodies for an academic conference, like this collection of college deans who are with us this morning (a very select breed of sinners, as we all know). And there should be a word for the deans from the Lord. But is this the wrong conference? Is this text for the Chicago Board of Trade or Wall Street? No, on this morning, this text is for deans, and for some others of you.

This is a text for you Marxists, who think the Bible is only about heaven, fairy tales and pie in the sky. This text says, Where is Abel, your brother? "But, I don't believe in the Bible." The Bible wants to know what you have done with your brother, where is he? His blood cries out from the ground.

And this is a text for you fundamentalists. You believe whatever it says, even if it says that a carp swallowed Jonah. That's fine, folks; now, where is Abel your brother, where are your little sisters and brothers holding up their empty bowls? That is what the Bible wants to know from you. What do you say?

"The hungry are somewhere else," you say, "and we are not grinding them. You will not touch us with that one, Elvee! You will not touch us unless you spiritualize the text!" Just

Greed

so! Who are the poor you are grinding? The nerd down the hall? The nasty waiting in your office on Monday? The benumbed fallen among college thieves?

Still, on this dark day of autumn rain, in a rural town surrounded by the great midwestern harvest, the poor we grind are in the farther world. They are the millions of starving in the Third World. We have given them much, but more is required. The problems of distribution are downright mystifying, but we must solve them. Our charity is in some places refused and our food lies rotting on the docks, but we must persevere. We may not forget that not so far away, under the same sun, within shouting distance of an airline, children with sunken eyes raise their empty bowls to you. You capitalists, you socialists have not managed to feed them yet. And you grind them too. You, Mother India, spend on weapons, shun your children. You, Father America, grind against every revolution. You don't ask whether, as in China, it feeds the people. You only know you are against it!

"I will not forget what you are doing," says the Lord."

CRY THE BEAUTIFUL BOYS

October 17, 1967

This is for the war dead! Cry our beloved country! Cry the beautiful boys! The gold is tarnished. Brought up in scarlet, they embrace shithills. The body you carefully clothed this morning, whose dull pressure you feel against the chapel seat (as the earth pulls you away from the sun) for them, does not exist. The mind, the strange and beautiful event in you, to which the universe has come after a long journey, is for them extinguished. The socket, the orifice, the auditory canal, from behind which like a shining god you see, hear, feel this burnished day in October, is for them, a vacancy.

Cry the beautiful boys, nor more lit by the sun; no more rolling with the sphere; no more pushed by the seasons, no more the great sea and the wind, no more the faded autumn road, no more the sweet pain of living. Their children will never stand on the earth. The legacy from parents they cannot use. So many faces will never happen.

So let the old men in Congress hear my cry! Your rhetoric cannot restore these boys their most precious gift—life. So let the war dissenters hear my cry: These dead have given you this day's cause, but what of them?

So let the chiefs of Wall Street hear my cry; let their fine women be silent in the great houses to hear my cry: You live off the dead!

Let the generals hear my cry: These were very young who fought for you. Many did not want to go. You say this war is in self-defense, but you are not convincing! When it is all forgotten, what will you have settled? What bright treasure will you show us that was purchased by all this life?

In a few years they will not be missed. There will be bodies to take their places on Saturday night in the theatres, on Sunday afternoon in the great stadiums. Though nearer to us in time, they will be more forgotten than the boys of '18 who have their rewards at football half-times. These will go unsung, forgotten for fighting a war they didn't want to fight.

Fought well, but there was nothing. These were very young, sirs, they deserved better, deserved to die for something better than an era outworn.

So just in this chapel hour, before they slip from view, leaving the temporary ache—in this minute before they are overwhelmed by obscurity—I raise this cry!

BURNING THE WEEDS:
ALL FLESH IS GRASS

A voice says Cry! And I said, What shall I cry? All flesh is grass, and all its beauty is like the flower of the field. The grass withers, the flower fades, when the breath of the Lord blows upon it.

—Isaiah 40:6-7

Yesterday all was a bluster. The clouds scudded across a grey sky. This year's leaves hurried along the college paths, driven like displaced persons on the roads of Europe. Out in the country last night there was no moon. The stars sparkled and swayed in the strong south wind. I searched for Andromeda through the glasses. There it was! Three hundred billion stars packed into the vague light of a single candle in the sky. Frail light in flight coming here for us? For God? For no one? Displaced?

The stars were the far away fires. Last night in the dark Lutheran countryside, there were nearer fires. It was a good night for burning weeds. I set fire to my roadsides and the wind whipped the flames into a furious storm that mowed down the weeds, twisting, crackling. They shriveled into black dust.

"That's pheasant cover, Chaplain!"

"I know, but it stops the snow, then drifts it over the road in winter."

"Always a choice, there's always a choice."

We burned and we thought. We thought of great world conflagrations, fires in the hearts of cities, Dresden, Tokyo. We thought of the tares philosophy mixes into the theological wheat which at the end of the world must be weeded out. We thought of our life as a fire burning in the weeds.

Only a few months ago weeds were pushing, struggling, climbing, endlessly multiplying magnificent green craving for light and space, weeds, swaying in the sun and the rain. Yesterday they stood around like dry old men, shivering, ragged, dusty, waiting to be swept up and thrown away.

There along the fencerow, in forgotten corners, they were not without names: Pig and Rag and Golden and Aster, and Joe Pye, blown across the November universe, settling down by fence posts, quietly dying under the snow, waiting like Lazarus in the dark and the cold, shooting up in the springing year, dancing the summer hours away in the lazy roadside breezes, ejaculating new seed in the shock of autumn storms, then gently, gently, not so gently, sliding down to death in the frosty pungent air, or rage, raging in the Chaplain's fire, in the breath of the Lord, blowing from the south at twenty miles an hour, last night, out in Luther's countryside under Kant's sky.

THE OLD PEACE OF GOD

My kindness shall not depart from you,
neither shall the covenant of my peace be removed.

—Isaiah 54:10

Only a few vessels were to be seen on the lake; and below me in the harbour all was very quiet. It was a wonderful picture: one could scarcely hope to see it today in quite the same mood. The landscape and the colours are indeed the same, but the magical peace which lay over it all is a thing of the past.

—Across the St. Gotthard in 1878

The peace of God. When it came it affirmed the landscape. It was the Yes of a Grandma Moses farmscape, cow and barn, haystack and summer field, autumn cloud and ducks in a pond, a flag and a train in the distance.

The peace of God. When it came, it came like a river in flood. Good things spilled out everywhere, grain and wine and fruits, springtime and harvest, houses and children. All was well. *All shall be well and all manner of thing shall be well.*

The peace of God. When it came, it came like a fresh spring morning. Like a friendship in fall. Like the beauty of the valley hills. Like a starlit night, like this careless leisurely day at college.

I sat out back of the barn last night amidst the weeds I'd not cut down last summer. The sky was filling with autumn clouds scudding along before a rushing wind. We sang of that wind this morning in St. Frances' beautiful hymn: "O rushing wind and breezes soft, O clouds that ride the winds aloft, Oh, praise him!" An autumn day was dying in the deep woods. The ducks came in over the farm, banking and landing on Oakleaf lake where some of your friends are popping at them this morning, as we pray for their safety. As the evening light failed, through the grass with noiseless tread came Issa Isabella looking for a woodpile. Isabella is a wooly caterpillar of real quality! Chocolate brown and ebony black, furry to the touch, she curls up in a little ball in your hand. She's been crawling through October like this since three million years before Jesus, seeking a cozy corner in which to sleep for the winter. When I saw her last night, I experienced the peace of God.

The peace of God, the old peace of God. It seemed as if, given sufficient time, it could pacify even the enemy in the dark, nature red in tooth and claw, the beast in the forest, all that dangerous, poisonous, chthonic other, and make of them one kingdom, one peaceable kingdom.

The peace of God. When it withdrew, the land failed. No water came to the wells. There was no grass and the cow forsook her calf. The wild creatures stood on the bare heights, panting for air. Their bodies failed. The prophets still prophesied peace, but there was no peace. Nothing was well.

The peace of God. Once it came to an old priest. Summer and winter he took his turn at temple duties. He waited for it to come. It seemed as if it might not come. Then there was the mid-winter day during the festival when they stood there, the parents with the child. He took it in his arms. This was it. His old heart sang: "Lord, now let your servant depart in peace, for my eyes have seen your salvation." That child grew up to be a wandering teacher of the people. The peace of God was in his teaching. Blest are those, he said, who make peace. It was very important to him.

The night before they crucified him, when he shared bread with his friends, and wine was passed around the table, there was peace in the room, clouds and thick darkness along the ways of life, but peace there, and God.

The old peace of God, it still comes, out behind the barn on an autumn Saturday night, here at the Lord's table on an autumn Sunday morning.

REQUIEM FOR A COACH

Born seventy-eight years ago on a farm in Iowa, the eldest of five children. His mother died when he was young, and he was, very early, on his own. He lied about his age to join the Navy during the first War, the only lie, I think, he ever told in his life. After the war he went off to Upper Iowa College with five dollars from his father in his pocket. He studied the sciences, played football, peeled potatoes in the kitchen, and each evening lit the lamps of the town to earn his way. He was to light lamps all his life for somebody out there in the dark.

Then, first teaching jobs in Iowa and Minnesota. He met Angie in Preston, Minnesota, where she was a school teacher. There was a master's degree from the University of Minnesota and finally a long and not-to-this-day-forgotten tenure in Waseca High School as teacher of the sciences, coach and friend to generations of high school youth. He came up to the hill, the Gustavus hill, in 1949, and for 21 years was educator, trainer, coach, counselor, friend and father to generations of students and colleagues, many of whom gather in this hour to bless his memory.

During the first eleven Gustavus years, Lee and Angie were houseparents at Uhler Hall. We don't call them that anymore; we now say "head resident." But that would not have described what Lee and Angie were: in-house parents who mothered and fathered and disciplined and encouraged and succeeded! How many of us have tried our hand at it over the years and no one has bettered the Kroughs! Their record remains in the collective memory of the college.

And the horizons were always larger than the college: the soft winds of the Giants' summer fields; the Lodge; the Rotary Club and the Presbyterian Church—he never missed a meeting of any of them. Through the American Legion, he gave twenty-five years of service to the best scholars, athletes, and future civic leaders among the young men of Minnesota. For this he received the Legion's highest awards and the gratitude of thousands of young men and the respect of senators and college presidents. He belonged to the State Coaches Association, the National Track Coaches Association, the American Association for Health and Physical Education and many other societies.

At Gustavus he coached just about everything at one time or another: football, track, basketball, baseball. He was always stepping in somewhere, which was wherever he was needed. "He was a team man," Holly said yesterday. "He always gave more than was required." At the same time everything was placed in perspective. Coach Don Roberts said, "The man had his priorities straight. His family, his work, his community, his leisure. It all fit in."

He leaves behind Angie, his wife; Mary, Robert, James and their families; seven grandchildren, for whom he was not only the Compleat Angler but also the Compleat Grandpa! He was a father and grandfather to this family. But beyond that he was a father to so many people that these few words spoken by one must be a tiny island in the great sea of unspoken memories gathered in this room and throughout Minnesota today. There is not time to say very much of it. So it is that each of us is left in the quiet of the hour with private memories which we may say only to God.

Lee Krough was quiet and strong. He was good. He was kind. He was wise. You sought him out. You found him like a moth finds a streetlight on a stormy night. He steadied you. He made the impossible seem more possible, and you played *for* him, and you confessed to him. You told him things you wouldn't tell your own father. Amidst our fragmented and ineffective lives, he seemed whole, present, effective—and you wanted to be like him. You always knew where he stood. He didn't have to dominate you to change you. He was genuine, all the way through, a gentleman. He stood tall, he 'carried' himself. He was disciplined, honest to a penny, humble, dignified, no phony, except, as Kyle Montague has it, except when he worked hard to be angry with the players. It never did work, for anger in him was the transparent wispy cloud passing over the continual sunlight of the warmest disposition. He was a man of deep reserve, so he didn't always say what he was thinking, but you knew when you had it wrong, or weren't making it on the issue. There was a sudden flush and grin, then you grinned, and you went on.

We must go. . . . Yet, before we do, we must say something about Angie, because Lee would have it that way. A few years ago when he was inducted into the Football Hall of Fame, that is what he wanted especially to say, that he received from her the supreme and singular gifts of life and home and support (the late suppers when one came home weary from the fields of work). He'd not have been much to others without her. He said it. She was his life.

The images from the last years are filled with all the color of life and contentment: hunting and fishing, and football games with Todd, and travels with Angie, and Pfeffer with friends on Wednesday night, and driving for the community center, and helping everywhere and everybody, and the quiet evening hours too, watching a game or reading a book.

He was a man who spoke a few words but read many. He was reading when the end came. He read most of Aleksandr Solzhenitsyn's books in recent years. I appreciated that fact when I heard it, because something spoke to me when Angie said it. Solzhenitsyn's God is like I thought Lee's God to be: never to be used as an excuse for human irresponsibility, nor to obscure truth or justify senselessness; nor in whose name one said something against another while loving oneself, but rather, a living God, ineffable, unfathomable, who liberated one's natural life from everything pseudo-religious and pseudo-Christian. That is how it was for Lee.

A last picture. It was at St. John's a few years ago, in the heat of a ferocious struggle when a Gustie lineman limped to the sidelines, and found Lee, and while Lee was fixing him indicated that he didn't very much want to go back in. Lee thought he should, that he was all right, mostly frightened. That lineman went back in, found the courage for it, and stood taller the next day. It was something like that the other night at the hospital. The struggle was not easy and Lee had come over to the sideline for a few hours, but the signal was,

"Go back in," and courageously Lee went back in, back out onto the profound playing fields of God. Give him eternal joy, O Lord, and may your light rest on him forever. *Amen.*

Lee Krough, Associate Professor of Physical Education, longtime assistant football coach and trainer at Gustavus Adolphus College, died August 25, 1977.

NOVEMBER

LUTHER AND HIS MOM

The fear of the Lord is the beginning of knowledge, but fools despise wisdom and instruction. My son, forsake not the law of your mother.

Essence of winter sleep is on the night. My November guest is near. It's pumpkin time. Allhallows' Eve and cozy stories of Luther and Katy suggest themselves, or Luther and his dog, or Luther and Faust in Auerbach's cellar. Or how about Luther and his mom?

Now Gusties, Luther's mom was the better sort of mom, a supermom, a real quality mom, a well-situated mom. Don't be fooled by Lucas Cranach's painting of her, where she looks like Luther, a swarthy, peasant lady of dour countenance. Luther insists that she beat the tar out of him for stealing a simple nut; that she used to go around the house singing: "No one cares for me and you. That's my fault and your fault, too." But Dr. Luther has left us with the wrong impression. What you need to know is that her first name was Marguerite (they called her Hannah), but of more consequence, her last name was Lindemann. The Lindemanns were well-situated people. They were not your average Lutheran peasants from southern Mower County. The Lindemanns lived in Eisleben. That is like living in Rochester! Luther's maternal grandfather and uncles were the professional elite of that city. Educated at the unversity, they were lawyers, doctors and politicians. Some of them lived on pill hill in Eisleben.

Luther's father, Hans Luder, was from Moehra. Moehra was like a little Norwegian town outside Rochester without much class. Hans was climbing up the social ladder when he married Hannah. He made his move by going into the mining business in Mansfield, with a little financial help from his new in-laws. Hans planned that his oldest son, Martin, would continue the upwardly mobile trend in the family by becoming a lawyer, consummating marriage into honor and wealth, making them all disgustingly rich. So you can understand that when Martin suddenly dropped out of law school and entered the seminary, the old man flipped. He was very aggravated. The exchange between father and son was so hot, that it has not cooled down after 450 years. Today a famous Harvard psychologist explains Luther's whole psycho-history as a reaction to his father.

Eric Erickson's *Young Man Luther* was written before the women's movement. We see better than Erickson that Luther was, in fact, a mother's boy. Aren't most clergy? Luther used to say "My daddy worked in the mines, and my mother carried wood on her back." That's what he told the rich dandies from Rome who were sent by the Pope to reprimand him for his loose talk. Luther had considerable investment in his own improbability vis-a-vis Rome. Here was a peasant from the German sticks standing up to all the fashion of Rome. How would you like to have been that boy's mother? He gave her no credit.

Actually, she didn't mind. She enjoyed it, even when a book was published, outrageously claiming that she had been a maid in an Eisleben bath house. The book claimed that on a Shrove Tuesday, a handsome young man in red clothing visited her and got her pregnant, and then married her off to a local businessman. The handsome young man was the devil. Her first born the anti-Christ, Luther.

After Luther joined the faculty at Wittenberg, she took a real liking to his faculty colleagues, Amsdorf and Melancthon—the whole clique who gathered on Friday afternoons at Whiskey River to discuss the prince, the Pope and the Gospel.

Her best friend was Phil Melancthon the future 'preceptor of Germany' who was Professor of Greek, the Jack L. Clark of Wittenberg University. When she came to Luther's house for weddings or christenings, she preferred conversing with Dr. Phil. He in turn paid her a wonderful compliment. ''Nobody could speak and sing as Luther later did if he had not first heard his mother's voice.''

For a fact, no one in twenty centuries of church history would sing like Luther—not Augustine, Aquinas or even Karl Barth. If the world ends soon, nobody ever will. His hymns, his devotional pieces, his sermons, his commentaries, even his aggravated letters—sing! Hans Sachs called him the ''Wittenberg Nightingale.'' We have but to note today the feminine accent and metaphor in that song. Listen to Martin. ''Faith with open arms embraces Christ. Faith holds the hand out, the sack open, and lets him do nothing but good. Faith is given when you open your mouth and hold still, and let yourself be filled. Faith is a tender, precious thing, and easily injured.'' And in his treatise *Magnificat,* Luther speaks of all our senses as ''floating in God's love, and being saturated with divine sweetness.'' Submissiveness, earthiness, imminence, nurture, ecstasy—this is the Luther ''anima.''

''Even if you are feeble,'' he wrote, ''and soil yourself like an infant, God will not throw you away, but will always clean you and make you better. God is pregnant with us, gives birth to us, nurses us.''

''I will not desert you,'' says God, ''I am the womb that bore you and I cannot let you go.''

Let us pray: O God, Mother, you are the nest of this November day. I sing a song to your last golden fingers in the high branches, a song of winter coming on, of the little birds seeking shelter, coming home now. I'm coming home now, Mother. *Amen.*

LUTHER AND HIS DOG

*Then he said to Tobias, "Get ready for the journey, and good success to you both."
So his son made the preparations for the journey. And his father said to him, "Go
with this man: God who dwells in heaven will prosper your way, and may his angel
attend you." So they both went out and departed, and the young man's dog was with
them.*

—Tobit 6:16

This tale about the boy Tobias, his angel and his dog, going out the door and down the road,
was one of Luther's favorites—Rembrandt's too; you may still see his sketch of it. You may
not have learned this story in Sunday School because the Protestants removed it from the
Bible after Luther died. But Luther thought it was a wonderful story and a very sensible
book, useful for teaching fathers and mothers the art of Christian home management! This
had become a concern of Luther's after he married the runaway nun Katherine von Bora
and set up housekeeping himself.

Apparently our Lord and the disciples didn't keep a dog in the house at Capernaum. Despite
the Renaissance painters' inclination to include dogs in our Lord's life, there is no indica-
tion that Jesus kept a dog. He didn't keep a wife either, and the clergy didn't marry for
a thousand years in imitation, until Luther fixed everything by marrying his Katy. The dog
must have come into the house with the children. "That," said Soren Kierkegaard, "was
a great defeat for Christianity." The Lutheran pastors lost their singleness of heart to wives,
dogs, gardens, stuffy front room parlors. The breviary and the monastery garden were ex-
changed for the grocery cart and cans of Ken-L ration. Just last week I watched my son
go out the door with his angel and his dog to get the mail.

After the dog came into the house, it was Katy who wanted the dog to sleep in the courtyard, but Dr. Luther wouldn't hear of it. The dog shall stay in the bedroom!

"Look at that dog," he once remarked, "There is nothing wrong with his whole body. He
has glistening eyes, stout legs, beautiful white teeth, and a good stomach." (Luther had a
bad stomach.)

"For a fact," said Luther, "this dog proves that God makes common to all life his best gifts."

"I wish I could pray the way that dog looks at meat."

Would this dog go to heaven? "Certainly," said the reformer, "God will create a new earth
and new dogs with hides of gold and fur of silver. God will be all in all and we will play
with the snakes." There may not be any Baptists in Luther's heaven—he once threw a Bap-
tist out of the house for asking a question he couldn't answer—there would be dogs and
snakes.

Today we smile at Luther and his dog, who are destined to meet in heaven, yet many of
us agree with Luther that animals belong to our ethical universe. They are not machine
parts without pain or purpose, or suffering or joy in living. "I am life which wills to live,
in the midst of life which wills to live." Those are the words of the Lutheran missionary,
Albert Schweitzer. Over the bed into which Schweitzer fell each evening, tired from a long
day of medical practice against great odds in the African jungle, hung the picture of Charles
Darwin.

A certain science can inform me how my dog is put together; it does not inform me as to what my relationship to my dog ought to be. That requires another language, a language which Darwin also knew. Very thoughtfully he wrote in his journal: "If we choose to let conjecture run wild, then animals, our fellow brethren in pain, disease, suffering and famine—our slaves in the most laborious works, our companions in our amusements—they may partake of our origin in one common ancestor—we may be all netted together."

Luther would have understood. We should too.

THRICE HAIL, GUS

I used to be able to sit in this chapel and see all the way to the row of great conifers that borders Resurrection Cemetery. Many buildings have risen in between now and one must stand to the south beyond Schaefer to see those sentinel pines. Under those trees many of our dear colleagues and friends are buried. The grand lady, Bertha Vickner of Vickner Language Hall, and Al Peterson who lived in a shack behind the stadium, who crafted exquisite violin cases. He gave them away to music students. And Candy Hall, student, member of the Symbionese Liberation Army. And Prof. Evan of Anderson Theatre, and Prof. George who taught literature for thirty-seven years, much loved. This week an old coach came home: Gus Young.

> Thrice Hail, Gus,
> Coming home now,
> Through an old Minnesota day.
> By the roadside, still the aster,
> Purple aster, paler now.
> Still the leaves in oak and aspen,
> Browning now, browning now,
> Falling now,
> A generation coming down.
> Though each, a single
> Death route
> Taking,
> Gliding, turning,
> Breaking,
> Branch on branch,
> All are gathered in eternal
> Gardens
> Waking

Verl J. (Gus) Young, basketball coach at Gustavus Adolphus College from 1949 to 1957, died October 31, 1977.

NOVEMBER 22, 1963

Who if I cried would hear me among the angelic orders?

—Rainer Maria Rilke

Sometimes things so permanent in worldthis
As always be in place
Familiar learned to accept
Daycome seasonchange
Summersmile after springchill
Like great tree stood at roadsturn
Where passing glad often.
Then, great storm!
Darkwind towndown and tree fall.

Tree shaking!
Tree   fall.

Calm, Washington,
Gone home evening
Larger place
Than Washington
Taller town.

BEARD

The word of the Lord came again unto me.

—Jeremiah 1:4

Beard is dead. Only yesterday he attended a wedding dance, merry and bright. But there he felt a trembling, so that he must return home, go down, his knees to kiss the earth. He was to feel his blood boil, his bones ache, his faculties decompose. It was time to try his strength. The mouth once opened in song, must vomit now; God was in a groan. The pain was pungent, but he laid his strength upon it. He did not smart; he strove earnestly until it was not to be. He was a profitable servant.

Watching hands transplanting
Turning and tamping,
Lifting the young plants with two fingers,
Sifting in a palm-full of fresh loam,—
One swift movement,—
Then plumping in the bunched roots,
A single twist of the thumbs, a tamping and turning,
All in one. . . .

Beard was honest, like plants,
A seed upon the wind
Settling down among autumn bodies,
Waiting like Lazarus
In the cool and the dark,
Shooting up in the springing year
Dancing the summer hours
Feeling the shock of autumn
Hastening the mortal ripening,
'Til gently, do not go gently—
Ragged, dusty,
Sliding down
In the frosty air
Waiting,
Like Lazarus

The first word came in September in St. Joseph's Hospital, Mankato. *Honor your doctor, in those things that concern him. Do not refuse his prescriptions for fear of outcome.* The second word came in October at St. Mary's Hospital, Rochester. The leaves fell from a garden far away. *Drink this cup. It is yours.* The third word came in November in Methodist Hospital in Minneapolis. The day was cold. Wick was there, and Moose and Sam, and Beard's mother. *Your eye is bright like an Advent candle! By his holy anointing may you be forgiven.* The penultimate word came yesterday at the evening meal. *Go to God along the ganglion, go.*

Douglas (Beard) Sandberg, associate director of admissions at Gustavus Adolphus College, died November 16, 1974, at the age of 26.

DECEMBER

EXAMINATION BEFORE CHRISTMAS VACATION

The Old Dean

Kant did not, like Rousseau, go to Holy Communion, did not, like Lessing, call Luther to witness. Instead, when the University of Konigsberg was proceeding in solemn procession from the great hall to the church for the University service on the Dies Academicus, Kant used ostentatiously to step away from the procession just as it was entering the church, make his way round the church instead, and go home.

—Karl Barth

There was an old dean around Gustavus, four deans back, Dean Albert Swanson, who sat in the last row of chapel every day. Because he was a "regular," he also observed that on these days before examination, certain students were present for the first time. He never failed to mention this to me along the walk. He thought they'd come for special assistance. It was also his opinion that they should receive it. That's grace!

Grace was not my original intention today. I was thinking about Christmas vacation and how much I deserved it. I thought of Albert this morning, however, so, in his memory, I appeal to you. My dear friend! Don't despair! Don't be cynical! Don't be discouraged! Do the best that you can, with what you have. Resign yourself to the results as God's will. Leave the rest to the devil! Keep going!

After the old dean, another came who was soon after killed in Vietnam. He was sent there by the U.S. government with other educators, to pacify the villages. It worked in America. Why didn't it work in Nam? His helicopter went down near DaNang.

The next dean was quite sophisticated. He read the *New Yorker* and clipped the *Times*. He came to chapel only on ceremonial occasions. Many of his patterns are still imitated by the faculty.

The present dean is like the old dean. He is a chapel "regular." He's even moved up ten rows from the back. He laughs out loud. The Kingdom goes forward, friends! Perhaps you will do well on your examinations this year. *Amen.*

ADVENTUS DOMINI

Advent!
The time before Christ.
Time of longing in a fallen world.
Time of waiting in a damp autumn room,
   when nobody comes.
The happy song of Pentecost, of Harvest,
   dies with summer in the trees,
   the coming of the lively snow.
The neighborhood is deserted,
   we are alone.
To thee, we exiles, children of Eve, lift our crying
To thee, we are sighing as mournful and weeping
We pass through this vale of sorrow.

Advent!
Somewhere behind the good life
   into which we have come,
somewhere behind the banquet and
   the basketball,
Is pain, sickness unto death,
The eternal stranger.

Advent!
Not again of Dachau and Hiroshima;
there is a darkness in us, I know.
Do not tell me of Dachau and Hiroshima.
Tell me if there is any possibility.

Advent!
Do not be afraid of the darkness!
Do not be afraid to wear the purple,
   shed the tears,
On the way to Christ.
O dayspring, splendor of the eternal light,
   and sun of righteousness.
Come and enlighten those who sit in darkness
   and in the shadow of death.

Advent!
Time of penitence and melancholy.
Quiet despair of December and snow.
Time before Christ,
Hushed expectation,
Quiet, waiting
For joy.

Tree

JANUARY

NOW THE ANIMALS GO TO SLEEP

This is a sermon for this Epiphany Day. It is also about the Christmas cards you received this year with the Christ-child set in the midst of the animals, not only the traditional cattle and sheep, but also butterflies, frogs and birds. Beyond that it is a dialogue between myself, my two-year-old daughter and you, the pew sitter. Of course, at two years my daughter doesn't understand this sermon and doesn't need to. So this is for you. Now the animals go to sleep.

Pastor Daddy: It is winter, Stephanie. Now the animals go to sleep. A month ago they scurried where the fall trees rustled and the late flowers bloomed. Now everything is still. Snow and bitter winds clamor over the field, and the backyard's as dead as the moon.

Stephanie: Where are the animals gone, Daddy?

Pastor Daddy: They're gone to sleep in eggs, and chrysalis and cocoon. They're tucked away in crannies in the bark of the tree. They are snuggled under the cover of leaves and snow. The toads are sleeping in the mud.

Pew Sitter: Whoa, Donner and Blitzen, whoa, Pastor! Don't waste my church time on animals and insects and snow! There isn't any snow in heaven, or everlasting frogs under the mud of eternal farm ponds.

Pastor Daddy: Quiet, old Pew Sitter! This sermon isn't for you. It's for my daughter Stephanie. It's for children who don't understand it and don't need to. I'll proceed with my sermon. I was passing through Bernadotte Library last week, where all of my sermons are stored in books. There must be two hundred years' supply, though ten more will take me through. You're itching to get out of here in four, I know, and will not even hear the decade through. No matter, it will never all be told anyway, all of it, not even if I stay a hundred years. I'll proceed with my sermon. I was passing through the library and there was a display board with a Christmas scene on it. A paper collage with a manger at the center bordered by animals, trees and stars. Created by librarians, no doubt, who in college took Introduction to Philosophy. In any event, placed around the baby God were a brown deer, a white rabbit, a black skunk with a white stripe, and a green turtle.

Pew Sitter: O dear! What would a baseball-capped, dog-leashed biologist with his Linnaeus under his arm have said of that?

Stephanie: Were there any skunks in Bethlehem, Daddy?

Pastor Daddy: No, honey. King Herod was a skunk, but he lived in Jerusalem.

Stephanie: Were there any turtles in Bethlehem?

Pastor Daddy: I don't think so, child. If there were, they'd have been asleep in the mud. They'd never heard the cry of the child, or seen the glitter of angels' silver wings.

Pew Sitter: But shouldn't this natural mistake have been called to the attention of the librarians?

Pastor Daddy: Of couse not, old Pew Sitter. With stories it's quite proper to rearrange nature. Even to go so far as to create a star that dances along the fence posts leading the wisemen to the place. Karlis Kaufmanis comes here each year to convince us that this star is a natural conjunction of planets and follows natural laws. No way, Jose! This isn't an astronomer's star. This is a poet's star. It does acrobatics. It stops at night so the wisemen can rest. In the morning it cameltrots along the road to Bethlehem. This star belongs to poets and to children.

Stephanie: What about the animals, Daddy?

Pastor Daddy: I don't know who put the animals on the board, nor for that matter who wrote them into the Christmas story, but it was a wonderful thing for them to do. It made it possible for them to become godly. This is a surprise, really. The early Christians weren't much interested in animals. Take St. Paul for example. He didn't much care for animals.

Pew Sitter: Once he was bitten by a snake.

Pastor Daddy: That's correct, Pew Sitter. You do know your Bible! Do you also remember that he talked about cows? He once quoted God as saying in the Torah, ''You shall not muzzle the mouth of the ox that treads out the corn.'' But then he spoils it by saying that God doesn't care for cows. Instead he inspired that sentence so that someday Christian ministers would get paid.

No, honey, the early Christians weren't interested in nature for itself. They owned so little of it, and it was passing away. So they created for themselves a heaven without crickets to which to go.

One day, however, there would be Christians as rich as Sadducees. They would own great estates, lands and animals. They would see the birds and beasts of their fields and woods and they would decorate their manger scenes with the landscapes of Italy, the fir tree woods of Russia, the animals of the forest, the creatures of country lands and village streets. These Christians have a heaven where it isn't light all day and all night too. In it, snow falls in a darkening wood, and geese get up out of a cornfield in the cold. ''I am about to go on a long journey,'' one of them said, when he was dying. ''I expect to see my Lord, but also many curious animals.''

We are more like these Christians, Steph, so we place around our Christ-child all of these things we value. Old Pew Sitter, we will leave the library display just as it is!

Stephanie: I like that, Daddy.

Pastor Daddy: O Stephanie, child, only yesterday you held out your little arms to catch the moon coming through your nursery window. You clutched your woolly bear and talked to it. You cried out with delight to see the cat Mittens appear in the doorway. You understand this Epiphany day that the Christ-child was visited by dromedaries with steaming nostrils.

Tomorrow, you will forget all this. You will be grown up. You will sit in a house to play cards with your friends—talk of taxes and movies, business and funerals. When you die, the Lutherans will send you to a large room without snow, without animals.

Today, Epiphany day, the earth calls, the farmyard is filling up with snow. Perhaps, too, you will remember such days, old winter days at the farm, when the animals went to sleep. If you do, the Christ-child, from his beautiful picture surrounded by butterflies and frogs, will bless you, will save you.

SERMON FOR THE AUD

We lost an old friend last night.
She went out toward Sagittarius,
In a great shower of sparks,
And fury of atoms' storm.
How bright she burned behind her hundred eyes!
Then, embered low and dim,
At last silent and empty and blind,
Nothing stared across the frosty hill.
She was gone.
Was there something?
Could we say whether there was something?
Next year's children
Will cross the lawn
As if it were never there.
It doesn't matter,
If we tell them of something.
They would never believe us.
The glory that was Greece.
They would never believe us.

They would not believe,
There was the glory of a song
That would never be sung.
The Frisbee shouters and leapers,
Years and years.

O where did you go, glory?
Sweet, sweet words.
I pressed you on paper.
Hoped you were good.
I was happy.
I will never know.
You are gone.
I will not see you out in front of me
Like trees.

But friends, a great wall of the Aud remains,
Standing in the winter light,
A skeleton of herself,
Elegantly neo-classic;
Fire has made a simpler, more beautiful body.
The trash is gone.
I see a courtyard. I hear music under the stars.
I hear the wind whistle in the upper stories.
Amphitheatre!
Must you pull it down?
Why?

On January 8, 1970, the Gustavus Adolphus Auditorium, which contained the Chaplain's library, burned down.

An Old Friend

FREE FOR NOTHING OR FREE FOR SOMETHING?

To proclaim release to the captives . . . to set at liberty those who are oppressed.

—Luke 4:18

This is a liberation text! Did I freely offer to preach it? The problem is that I'm opposed to these liberation movements! Women's liberation? No way, Germaine! That's how you lose your servant secretaries and your servant wives. And if they serve you, it's always with a bloody reservation. Student liberation? No way, Jerry! That's how you end up with students uninterested in classics and dismayed by history. Third World liberation? No way, Omar! That's how you end up with little thought-control dictatorships and ruined economies. Academic liberation, Elvee? Hold on now, I need that one for myself! What if the church said I shouldn't teach my Hegel because he was a pantheist and tried to have his Infinite Spirit finitely human? Christian liberation, Elvee? Yes, a little of that too. And it's the Christians who ought to be liberated from their little despotic Christs. Everything is bound and nothing is loosed!

I was amused by the reaction of my Roman Catholic colleagues to "Sister Mary Ignatius Tells It All To You." They became very excited when they saw the play in the Gustavus coffee house last Saturday night. They were tyrannized by nuns at age seven and they can still feel it deep down. But my experience as a Protestant child wasn't any different. I shall never forget what seemed like the freest day in my life. It was a brilliant June Sunday; I was biking around Lake Calhoun in Minneapolis during the church hour. The people I knew were in church! I was out with the sparkling water, park benches, Sunday papers. I decided that I would be an atheist. Atheists, by my definition, didn't have to go to church, didn't have to believe everything in the Bible, could sin without guilt, could swear out loud and chew tobacco, have lustful thoughts—I was free!

As it turned out, after many years, this was only the second freest day of my life. There was a day when I walked back into the church, freely walked in; began slowly, sometimes painfully to take my place and my responsibility for the world as gift. Thirty years later, I can say that this was the freest day of my life.

That's the point of my title this morning. You can't just be free for nothing, that's not freedom. You have to be free for something. The other freedom is a false freedom, a negative freedom, an incomplete freedom. You have to be free for something, to be really free.

But free for what, Elvee? Freedom to become yourself. Of course! Freedom creates a context in which you can become yourself. So you free yourself from your parents to become yourself, and then you can freely adopt them as your parents and there begins a new relationship between you, a freer relationship. So you free yourself from other social relationships, even from the church, to become yourself, then, you can form these relationships again, but on another foundation, autonomy.

The danger of any liberation is that you may never re-form the relationships. You might become the *only* person. You might become the center of everything—God. There may not be anyone else or anything else except what you want, what you are, the way you see things.

But this is not freedom. This is alienation. A society in which everyone is free to be a single self is a society in which no one is either free, or oneself. This is negative freedom. This is freedom for nothing—*"Nada, nada, nada,"* the alienated Hemingway writes. Positive freedom is that you are freely together with the other. It is ultimately you for the other. It is you becoming the other, taking responsibility for the other, for something like marriage or the Church, even something like philosophy.

"You are called to freedom," writes St. Paul in his Letter to the Galatians, "and so, being called to freedom, become servants of one another." If you want to know how free you are, ask yourself a single question: For what are you willing to be responsible? If the answer is "nothing," you are not free.

Dear Gustie friend—you are here in Christ Chapel this morning. I see you. Why are you here? Are you freely here? Are you here because you have to be here? Are you here because somebody told you that you should be here? Are you here because you are afraid not to be here? Are you here to go to heaven or get a job?

Are you here because you want to be here? Because you like to be here? Here together with the other—people and music and spirits and candles, and books and bread?

I am here because I want to be here. I enjoy it here. It's the freest hour of the week for me. I love to be here because you are here and the Spirit in you speaks to me and frees me from myself. There are folk here because of their parents, or because of the temperature of hell, but they are not enjoying it so much. It shows in their demeanor and in their pinched expressions and clenched hands.

Sometimes I can see them from this pulpit despite my failing eyes. They are not singing the hymns. They are glowering at the readers, and I wonder about them. Why are you here? You were not glad when they said to you, let us go to the house of the Lord. What do you want? You don't have to be here!

It is that way with college too. It will be the freest day of your life when you finally take responsibility for being at Gustavus. When you can say I'm here because I want to be here, not for my folks, not for a job down the way, not for the neighbors or the relatives. Then you're free. Every semester we ask some of you to sit out for a while. It's obvious you don't want to be here. You're smart enough, but you're not here for your own reasons. There are all sorts of other things. So you need to go away, to find out what it is you want, what it is for which you are willing to be responsible.

When you know you want to be here, you're free. You can live with it. You can do something with it, even with these idiot classes and stupid friends.

Christ does this for us today. He frees and unites us. He does this if we hear his word and share his meal. He takes us, and blesses us, and breaks us and gives us to the world. The breaking is a breaking up of old ways and attitudes, a breaking free from that which holds us back. Breaking also makes it possible to be put together on a new foundation of freedom. When you are broken and freely given to others, you become very important to those others, who need to be broken and to receive the freedom. *Amen.*

FEBRUARY

FEBRUARY

And he entered the temple and began to drive out those who sold saying to them, it is written, my house shall be a house of prayer: But you have made it a den of robbers.

—Luke 19:45

It's jolly good to see you back on the hill, dear people. With joy we open this great house again, and we turn on the lights even if it's expensive this year. It's good to see the human figures hurrying along the walks. If this day doesn't have as much excitement as the beginning of the school year, it has its own matured excitement.

There are many leaden Lenten days ahead, but they can be endured. We have to see how the winter sports will come out. Any titles for the Gustie teams? And we have to hear the Allegri "Miserere" on Ash Wednesday. We have to celebrate the Gustavus Mardi Gras, Frost Weekend. There is a friend who must be taken out to dinner, a fraternity to be pledged, an experiment to be finished, a book to read. There is a familiar routine into which to settle. Since there are no freshmen around, no beginners, we look about us and see faces which we remember seeing way back before Christmas. We say, "Hello, how are you doing? Were you here winter term? Were you in Hawaii? Were you in Madrid? Where did you get the tan?"

Today, Jesus comes back to the house too, and he is very angry. He dares to say, the house is being abused. Some money changers have set up tables in the house, on the pretense of doing the business of the house. He attacks them and drives them out. He won't let them hawk their goods in the courtyard of the house. "Is it not written," he says, "my house shall be called a house of prayer for all nations, but you have made it a den of thieves."

This college is a great house, a house of thought for all nations. It exists for that purpose, and it belongs to all who serve that purpose. The old master Aristotle bequeathed his college, the Lyceum, to posterity with just such a description: "The garden, and the walk, and the houses adjoining the garden, all and sundry I give and bequeath to such of our enrolled friends as may wish to study literature and philosophy there in common, on condition that no one alienates the property or devotes it to his private use, and so that they hold it together like a temple in joint possession and live as is right and proper on terms of familiarity and friendship."

Do we not hold this garden and house together like a temple? We do. Here we think and argue and reflect in a community of friendship and familiarity. Here we are free. We may say what we think. In this temple, however, there are money changers. Some who appear to be doing us a service, but are actually robbing us and so are thieves. They sit in my office with materials for sale that offer the latest techniques for processing students toward jobs or Jesus. Behind the material is not tradition of inquiry, little that is scholarly, little commitment to anything other than the success of some short cut to somewhere.

When you drive them out, they protest. "We have three hundred colleges where this is working!" You are a money changer! Get out! Sell it to the church. Sell it to business. Sell it to Washington. Get out of this temple!

We are also in a house of prayer. This house is chapel to a larger house, the house of thought. On this day, at the beginning of term, we remind the larger house to be about its true business. Thinking is as divine as prayer. Many years ago, I studied with the philosopher A.C.M. Ahlen at Northwestern Seminary in Minneapolis. His favorite philosophers were Leibnitz and Aristotle, and he used to press them upon us. We wanted something more applied, like how to gain new members for the confirmation class, or how to do a liturgy correctly.

I can still see him walk to the window, gaze out, finger his moustache. I can still hear him say, "Gentlemen, thinking is also the worship of God."

TRANSFIGURATION

Sunday after the death of Randy Frerichs, a junior pre-medical student from Rochester, found dead in his room in Uhler Hall, February 12, 1983.

My brothers and sisters: We begin a new college term. For some of you, the last term around. Where did the years go? For others of you, your first legitimate term at this college. Fall term was practice. That's how you explained it to your parents. But this one, you said, is for real! We are in the ball game now. That's good!

In mythic time this is Lent. Mythic time may be the only meaningful time. Time does not mean anything in itself; it requires to be gathered into paradigms by which we picture ourselves and our life in the world. In this mythic time we are on the threshold of Lent. On Wednesday you will be marked by ashes and you will hear the ancient words, *Memento mori,* Remember that you are dust and that to dust you shall return.

Lent once more. Lent means spring and tears. For the next seven weeks the readings from this lectern will tell of a personal journey, the journey of one soul through human suffering and human crucifixion which became all the human journeys everywhere. The suffering is the suffering of Jesus, but we will not escape it. He will become the example for us to follow. The readings will inform us that unless we suffer and die, we will be unformed and useless. The grain of wheat must die. Then it becomes many grains and is useful.

This death takes place every day, every moment. Every moment of life is a yield from death. We learn this as we participate in the life and death of others. It is not just another student, but *our brother* who died in the dorm last week. It is *our* parents in Rochester who are grieving.

Perhaps you did not know Randy well. I did not. Through his friends I am beginning to know him as an excellent student, a good person and a brother. I do not know the meaning of his death. But I do know that because he was a good person, I must become a better person to share in his life and complete our common task as humanity.

Not *a* sister, but *our* sister has lost her way. We participate in other lives. We begin to discover our true life when we participate this way.

At the same time, why should everything have to suffer and die? We protest aloud and in silent anger against this view of life. Why should everything be founded on death? The scientists and the medical clinics say they can change this. They will make you live to be one hundred and thirty years old, and your children two hundred. No more early grief. The social scientists and the politicians say we can change society so that there are not a million people walking a road in Nigeria, sick, dying along the way from hunger. It can't be possible that we are passing away on a decaying star in a decaying social order. Why are we fighting in Central America? Why kill anybody with a better future coming from technology? But that future never seems to come. We just go on dying.

How many brilliant physicians and neurosurgeons and internists are there at the Mayo

Clinic, with their great arsenal of medicines and drugs—still they ultimately lose every patient to death.

Whether we like it or not, this is the nature of the world. It is built on death. This is the life we live and it is not likely to change. Not even the technology of the next twenty years will overcome death. It will only introduce more complicated ways to die.

All of this cannot be a reason to surrender to despair, to take refuge in distractions, gadgets, drugs. We can't use the facts to justify sickness, hunger, sadness. We have to fight against them—like your room over there in the dormitory. The fact that it's a mess is no reason not to clean it again.

Even so, why suffering and death? That's our final Why. We don't ask it every day. There are events like Randy's death that cause us to ask it. We have explanations, theodicies. Can we finally escape the idea that the agony of life is in the very life of God? That's how I see it anyway. I say to those who suffer, "Friend, this is the suffering of God," to those who are dying, "Friend, this is the dying of God." That is what we learn from Lent. God is out there on the human road! God is struggling! It is God who will die, and to all who in their suffering cry out, Why have you forsaken me? comes the response, "I am with you in it." Or, Why did this happen to me? "It is happening to me in you." We bear the image of God in our suffering.

In the gospel reading of today, Jesus is discussing these matters with Moses and Elijah. He speaks about his suffering with Moses. Moses suffered a stubborn reluctant people as political leader, took them to the promised land, then was refused entry himself. Jesus speaks of his suffering with Elijah. Elijah suffered the same people. Jesus is speaking about suffering and tasks amidst an erupting chaos, stones flying, guns firing, bread lines, job lines stretched out in the cold of a city morning.

As I read my *Time* magazine each week, this is the story of humanity. A story of people struggling and suffering. A tale of bloodshed and violence, of crime and throw-away children. It is into this story that God has come and stands by us now in the Christ. God suffers. The suffering of human history is God's suffering. God is handed over to the power of time, of history, of man. To suffer with him is to live the life we are living, victims and victimizers of each other:

> *Men go to God when he is sore bestead,*
> *Find him poor and scorned, without shelter or bread,*
> *Whelmed under weight of the wicked, the weak, the dead;*
> *Christians stand by God in his hour of grieving.*

While Jesus was talking about the suffering in which he was taking a new lead, he began to shine, brighter and brighter, whiter than the chapel walls, than the sun on a clear winter day. He became beautiful. The glory shone in him. They do not stand against one another: cross and resurrection. Resurrection comes by way of death. The suffering of Jesus will consist in his becoming the form of our hopes, in our struggle for integrity wherever we are. He becomes the very body of humanity in which this struggle goes on, and we belong to that body. It is the body in which we are present to one another in good times:

the bright hockey arena last night; this magnificent chapel with music, exquisite, beautiful; and bad times, that cold, empty room of Frerichs' over in Uhler Hall on a gray February Saturday morning when a sad, cold wind blew through us. *Amen.*

MARCH

SPRING LIGHT

Lenten Thoughts

That I may know him and the power of his resurrection, and may share his sufferings, becoming like him in his death, that if possible I may attain the resurrection from the dead.

—Philippians 3:10

Lenten thoughts:
That I may know him and the power of his resurrection,
that I may share his sufferings,
that I may become like him in his death,
that if possible,
I may attain the resurrection from the dead.
It was still winter.
The brightly lit ice arena of the state hockey tournament
filled up the Saturday afternoon television with bright colors.
The shouts of the crowd shook the room.
Then it was over. The afternoon suddenly became empty.
I went out the door for a walk on the road.
Surprise! There was a light in the fields,
an ancient spring light, unexpected, early.
That I may know him and the power of his resurrection.
That another winter was over, was my first thought,
My second thought, this begins the end of another college circuit.
Once more the lilac darkness down by Rundstrom
once more a different bird song in the campus yard,
once more all the trees in new green dress
budding under nights of spring stars,
once more the crack of the bat and a lazy afternoon of baseball
in a college season always too brief.
Once more a generation passing.

You, Gustie senior, that I may know you and the power of your resurrection,
that I may share your sufferings, becoming like you in your death.
Wait, where are you going?
Your eager faces, your intense faces along the walk,
dappled by windy suns in September,
immersed in the gloom of November rains,
sullen now in the overcasts of March,
passing now, that I may share your sufferings,
all the weary waiting,
many a heartache, ambition, trial, compulsion, uncertainty.
I am not ungrateful for your life's drama, this college chimera, this tender theater of
    dreams.
We smelled the roses,
but you are suffering some loss. . .you are dying, and so am I.

All this was a long time ago, I remember,
And I would do it again, but set down
This set down
This: were we led all the way for
Birth or Death? There was a Birth, certainly,
We had evidence and no doubt. I had seen
  birth and death,
But had thought they were different; this Birth was
Hard and bitter agony for us, like Death, our death.
We returned to our places, these Kingdoms,
But no longer at ease here, in the old dispensation
I should be glad of another death.

Another death? The end of this magic lantern consciousness,
the light goes out, the flight of the ghost from the machine,
  the soul from the body?
Becoming like him in his death? What would that be like?
The death of the empirical ego, the death of me, the death of "I" who speak to you
  from this pulpit?
The I who saw the stars back of Lund last night, becoming like him
  in his death,
the I who saw the light in the fields yesterday, becoming like him in his death,
the I who heard *Rosenkavalier* from a dorm window, becoming like him in his death,
the I who heard mother play "Songs My Mother Taught Me" when I was six,
  becoming like him in his death,
the I who feels the spring coming in, becoming like him in his death,
I who chew the body of Christ and kiss your lips,
I who plunge my hot hand into the Gregory font,
I whose fancy ranges over worlds, becoming like him in his death,
that if possible, I may attain the Resurrection.
Lenten thoughts.

GOOD FRIDAY

It is over now.
Jesus is dead, is dead.
Life must go on, somehow.
Pilate must dine at home
With his wife.
Read a little Virgil before bed.
In two hours
The lights at the ball park in Kansas City
Must be turned on.
The Good Friday fans
Must shout and drink beer.
To the west of this church,
The lights must come on
In the prairie towns,
Like June fireflies
Just before night.
And in the far cities,
Los Angeles, San Francisco,
In the bright lights of
Restaurant, theater, City Lights bookstore,
People must pretend that
On this eve, there are no shadows.

Here, on the side streets of St. Peter,
With the chill of winter still in the air,
The whine of a truck on the highway,
The voice of a child on another street,
We must turn on the light in the kitchen,
To eat the evening meal.
Later, we must sit in the front room parlor,
To watch the blue light flicker
From New York.
But on this night,
Carson will not us charm,
We will run to sleep, to die.

In three days, it will all be possible again!
Palestrina, Bach and Giocometti!
Baseball, Spring, and the Shouting.
By Monday, everything will be fine.
Everything will be good!

GOD'S BODY

Unless a grain of wheat falls into the earth and dies, it remains alone.

—John 12:24

Last week, I walked the streets of Philadelphia for three days, watching God's body become thirty-eight floors of fashionable condominiums on Rittenhouse Square. I heard God's sonorities become the Bruckner Sixth Symphony in the aging Academy of Music, and I saw Christ's face in the faces along the street, Blacks in color, Jews in wool, Italians in shimmer, and one evening, a Bach partita from a woman alone in an upper room of the Curtis Institute. She had a Venetian face.

I schedule trips like this during Lent, to get away from Minnesota, because in Minnesota spring is so far behind. When the hockey and basketball tournaments are over, when the beer and toots of St. Pat's day have faded and there are only these days in between, it's time to go away, if you can, so I did.

I returned last evening to be here for this Eucharist. I tell you, *unless a grain of wheat falls into the earth and dies, it remains alone.* We gather in this Christian assembly to present one another not only with our own little deaths, but with the deaths of our brothers and sisters everywhere in the world. There are many who suffer with Christ on this Lenten day, who carry the death of Christ literally in their bodies, whose way is sorrow. We must think of them. We must pray that they do not despair; that they will not be tested beyond their strength. Who are these who rise about us at our table—Salvadorans and Nicaraguans, government and guerilla, persecutors and persecuted have raised the sword to die by it. Lord, have mercy!

Many are younger than we. They hoped for justice from the violence, these boys with guns, who should be playing baseball these lengthening spring afternoons. Only last Sunday a communion or a confession. Now they die for government or revolution. What do they know? How could they know? Christ! You are dying in them, for what? Do they know it is you? They have struggled to find the path to identity, the path of discipleship.

Unless a grain of wheat falls into the earth and dies, it remains alone. If it dies, it becomes many grains. What possibly could that mean for us, for you? You were meant for this death from the time of your baptism. Your parents carried you to a font somewhere in Minnesota, and we priests marked your baby skin with a cross. We said, ''You have been marked with the cross of Christ forever.'' Your parents should have winced, grandmother should have trembled in her furs. They hope, naturally, that you were baptized into the good life without too much suffering. The Church does not see it this way. You must suffer. The sign of the cross is on you. You have been marked. Would you wipe it off if you could? Yes, yes, but you cannot! The sign of the cross is on you, and into which fellowship of suffering it will carry you I do not know, but there will be that community for you, for there is no cheap grace anywhere. Will you work toward reduction in arms and an end to this madness; or will you choose deterrence, so that you must count weapon for weapon because it is better to be neither dead nor red for awhile? I don't know which path will be yours. I see you in your youth and vigor, many of you still not committed anywhere—but all of you will die somewhere. I hope you will find something large in which to die. And when your hour comes, I hope you will remember the sign and not forget the words: "The fellowship of his suffering, the power of his resurrection." The Resurrection is the possibility of a meaningful death. That is what we are celebrating on this day of the Resurrection, with all of the recent dead coming in around our table as witnesses, to watch our lives, to see how we do it, to register the nails that hold us to lives of service and integrity. *Now is my soul troubled, and what shall I say, Father, save me from this hour. No, for this purpose I have come to this hour.*

OTHER VOICES, OTHER ROOMS

So they drew near to the village to which they were going. He appeared to be going further, but they constrained him, saying, Stay with us, for it is toward evening, and the day is now far spent. So he went in to stay with them. When he was at table with them, he took the bread and blessed, and broke it, and gave it to them. And their eyes were opened.

—Luke 24:28-31

*T*o an open house at evening, home shall men come,
To an older place than Eden.
I know what it is in this story that haunts me,
That pulls and tugs,
That gathers in my throat,
That waters in my eye.
I have been looking for that room,
That evening room in Emmaus.
All around is vast universal night, dark and empty.
I am seeking that little kitchen room,
Bright as truth,
Warm as love.

My life is hectic, disordered.
My life is greedy.
I have lost my way in Jerusalem.
The world is old and I am spent.
I am looking for two walkers,
Moving away from this place
toward a village.
I am looking for another wayfarer
Walking alone.
I am looking for the room where
They took supper together.
I am looking for the clean well-lighted room.

I think I was in the room when I was a child.
I think the room was in my parents house,
Where we gathered for the evening meal.
I hear my father's voice. He was a Protestant minister.
He told once how Jesus sat at evening,
At meal with his disciples.
He said that at the end of everything,
Jesus imagined that in the kitchen of the Father's house,
He and his disciples would meet again at table,
After the world had done its worst.

Sometimes it seemed as if I might have to leave the world,
To find the room again.
Sometimes when I sang an evening hymn
Full of childhood, sleep and death,
I felt a tug toward the room in the sky.
Perhaps one should go over now.
A table is set, the candles lit,
The guests ready to enter the room.
O Father!

There was something wrong in that desire.
I still had things to do, promises to keep.
It could be wrong to leave too soon.
The room must be found on an earthly street.

A room to which one could go,
And come back again.
One could go in to talk and rest,
Then come out to keep promises.

Nightfall in Emmaus, the day spent.
They sat at table.
They intended to host him, their guest.
He it was, though, who took the bread
And became the host.
He broke it, gave thanks to heaven.
The guests understood that it was not over.
It had begun, and this was the feast,
And this the room.

Here is bread about to be broken,
Here is wine to share.
Here are disciples around,
Hopeful.
Friends, I think this is the room!

APRIL

FRIDAYS AFTER THE RESURRECTION

These Fridays after the Resurrection in Minnesota,
Are everything they are cracked up to be.
Spring comes in fits and starts,
Promises unkept,
Downers after uppers.
Today, the sun is shining,
Christ is risen!
Tomorrow, April is
The cruelest month.
You wonder whether
Anything happened!
Where is the new life
On Saturday night
In a West Berlin disco?
Where is the new world,
On main street in Manila?
It is still Friday before
Resurrection, all over the world.
Not less so on the streets of St. Peter.
The chill of winter in the air,
The whine of trucks going down to Des Moines,
The voice of a child in a house.
Jesus is still dead.
We turn on the light in the kitchen
To eat the delivered pizza.
Later still in the front room parlor,
Watch the blue light
Flicker, flicker in the void.
Does it matter
If it's Twins 3, Mariners 2,
Or Mariners 3, Twins 2?
Distraught, we run to sleep,
To drink, to swallow, to die.

Where is the resurrection in all this?
How does it come?
Jesus, where are you now?
What are you now?
Are you dead?
Please be dead so we may forget you,
And live all this on other terms.

Jesus is dead, is dead.
They tried to make you too large,
As if you could change reality.
You don't seem to fit at all.

Friends, what intrigues me about the Resurrection stories,
Is that Jesus does not come back
On stage at Forest Lawn,
But through a sea mist over Swan Lake.
He appears on a road, like the muddy rut
I take home each day.
He appears as men are eating and drinking
In a room, reminiscing, replaying old games.

He appears in the middle of the old life,
In its temporality and fragility.
He makes the old life a new life.
It is seen in a new way now.
Palestrina, Bach and Giocometti,
Classes on Monday and a baseball game.
A paper on physical theory, a lecture on Kant,
An essay on James.

Ultimately it makes possible the facing
Of this life as destiny, as will of God.
Essentially it means to say to life,
"Here I am, I put myself at your disposal,
No bargains, no barter. What do you
Want me to do and be?"

It means more than being a dutiful student
Or a happy professor in this monotony.
It means to feel the quality of life
Independent of the demands you make on it,
Independent of what you think should come back
As dividends.
And all of this without any change in
The external circumstances.
This is the secret of the resurrected life.

It is lived from within, quietly.
Others cannot tell whether it is there or not.
These Fridays after the Resurrection.
Why isn't everything changed?
It is changed from within.
The life and glory of the risen Christ
Is not apparent to the world.
Luther often reminded us that we know that glory
In a hidden way, that Christians do not perceive it
By external senses.
Rather, you die, and your life is hidden with Christ in God.
The worldly part of us does not understand this.
There must be evidence!
The resurrected life is not only hidden to the world,
It is hidden to the Christian who lives it.
It comes as a gift of peace and grace
Whereby all things are received as gift,
So one does not despair,
And life is meaningful, valid,
And we are not alienated from our present
Social and cultural life.
To be sustained by such confidence is to look out on life
With a quiet eye, look out at this Friday after the Resurrection.

A DOORWAY IN TIME

Doubting Thomas

Now Thomas, one of the twelve, called the Twin, was not with them when Jesus came. So the other disciples told him, "We have seen the Lord." But he said to them, "Unless I see in his hands the print of the nails, and place my finger in the mark of the nails, and place my hand in his side, I will not believe."

—John 20:24-25

This text of the doubting Thomas never fails to excite the doubting Thomas in me, never fails to bring this closet agnostic tumbling out of the closet. I can't just sit back on this one, like an obedient child. I can't let it be. When the Lord says, "It is to your advantage that I go away," I think, "Oh, yeah?" When my father used to say, "This hurts me more than you," I thought, "Oh, yeah?" When Jesus says today, "You are more blessed if you have not seen, yet believe," I think, "O Lord, tell me about it. What a sop!"

Did Thomas really place his finger in the Lord's scars, or was it a hallucination? Was it a later story, somebody's sermon attempting to convince themselves and us (too far away from the event to know), that Jesus was real and alive again?

I, of course, don't get to see him, or to touch the scars with my fingers, but then I am more blessed because I believe without seeing. Well, it isn't good enough! St. Francis, twelve hundred years later, wanted to see the wounds and got them in his own hands. The same for me please! It's only another eight hundred years. Why not?

Are you saying you want your own private experience, Elvee, you and Francis? If Jesus walked into the rain-spattered room of this day in Minnesota with his bloody hands, and you saw him, would anyone else see him?

Brothers and sisters, I asked the sexton to lock the doors on the chapel this morning. What if the Lord came through the door now too, between the electrons and nucleus, and then calcified, reconstituted, atom for atom, organ for organ, for a few minutes as he did for Thomas, so that we could touch the scars? What does it matter that the body disappears a few minutes later, scars and all, sucked like smoke into the heavenly spaces as it was in Thomas' time. Where did it go, Thomas? Where did the body go? Does it matter? We saw it! We touched it! What was it you touched, Thomas? Was it corporeal? Was it a body? You say yes? If it was a body, Thomas, it was not the body we know, continuous with time and space, with a gut. Your Jesus-body appears in different places at the same time. That is not a local body! Your Jesus-body passes through a closed door and disappears—poof! into the air. This is not a local body, Thomas. You are referring to something else.

And, tell me Thomas, tell me about those scars. Where are they tomorrow morning when you're eating breakfast down in the Jerusalem market? Did they just fold up and disappear like the wind through the keyhole of that door?

I wonder . . . did Thomas ever doubt again, years afterward, doubt that he had touched the scars, wonder what the scars were, on that long journey to the East where he spent his last years? What were those scarred hands on the afternoon he lay dying in the street, having been thrust through by the spear of an Indian, dying, far, far away from that spring room in Jerusalem?

Doorway in Time

MCB

Did Thomas, who apparently once touched the scars, learn that the Lord in his Resurrection was a universal presence? If scars touched in a local room in Jerusalem disappeared into a local heaven, were they also touched under an Indian heaven? Thomas touched the Lord's scars in his own wounded side, where the spear went in, on the streets of the city of Madras, as the sun set on the Ganges.

One of the wisest things the Church father Jerome ever wrote was that in his Resurrection "Jesus dwelt in all places, with Peter in Rome, with Titus in Crete, with Thomas in India."

Fifteen hundred years later, Luther preached this text of ours today: "Jesus came and stood among them and said, 'Peace be with you.'" Luther interprets this text by spiritualizing it. "His coming to us is the word of peace, and his standing in our hearts is faith. That Christ stood in the midst of his disciples denotes nothing else than that he is standing in our hearts." So today Jesus comes into the human heart through a doorway in time, a doorway, not to the past, but to a level of reality freed from time. When we hear "Peace be with you" in this chapel room today, a presence comes through the door. This is the upper room. The hands once opened to Thomas are opened to us. The Resurrection is always beginning again; we do not have to find it by a search of the past. It is an experience here and now if we will begin to live in the Lord's peace.

You are young now. Time will take away from you many precious memories, but not this, for God is the beginning and the end of every time and every place, so that in the midst of this mysterious life, which entails so much suffering as well as joy, the doorways yield silently to the One who comes with peace, lives and dies in us, is never absent from the room again.

THE GOOD SHEPHERD

I am the Good Shepherd; I know my own and my own know me, as the Father knows me and I know the Father; and I lay down my life for the sheep.

—John 10:14-15

This image consoled your grandparents' generation, who did not believe their contemporaries H.G. Wells and Bertrand Russell, that the universe was without a consolation. Nor did they agree with Matthew Arnold that the world was a "darkling plain" which "hath neither joy, nor love, nor light, nor certitude, nor peace, nor help for pain." The world was the still water of a Midwestern town, lazy with the drone of bees and the soft moving curtains in high ceilinged parlors where the old pastors read, "The Lord is my shepherd!" The image comforted, inspired confidence, reinstituted the world as a land of dreams "so various, so beautiful, so new."

Even to them, after awhile, it seemed, somehow, nostalgic—something lost from the childhood of a nation, out along the prairie, gathering at the river, I hear America singing. Something from a more innocent time, now returning as a reminiscence in the antiseptic, very mechanized, specialized hospital room. There above the stack of *Time* magazines, below the television screen—still waters appearing, green pastures, paths of righteousness, the valley of the shadow, oil, and table, the house of the Lord, the Good Shepherd.

What did you do when they were dying, Pastor? You said, "I'm sorry." Is that all? No, you became the voice of the Good Shepherd and you led them out into green pastures. That's how it was with your grandparents. They doubted, they feared. But for them there was a transcendent image, a tender word. I have whispered into their fading senses, "Yea, though I walk through the valley of the shadow of death."

How is it for us? Did the old myth survive the guns of August, the lights out in Europe? Does the Shepherd's foot fall on a hot Chicago, Saigon, speak-easy street, or his staff touch bodies on Guam, or Iwo, or is his voice heard in Dresden or Hiroshima? The answer is Yes. It still works! The invisible Shepherd remains in the human heart. You were united to that invisible image in baptism, and if you have turned away in frustration or anger or pride or hate, the image calls after you. The Good Shepherd walks among the inmost silences of the conscience, the solitary paths of the psyche. Behind the image, the words, is a presence that carries and consoles us, the Good Shepherd.

TONY CRAWFORD

That's how it was with him. Spring coming on with first willow bud and robin's song and earth's odor. Each Lenten evening, Venus a bright lantern swinging over the campus fields. Then suddenly ice in April, the spring peepers in the swamp frosted for their desires, so quickly was the frost of death on him, and he must through rain, through snow, through tempest go.

He faced it with courage and hope, but the illness was rapid, and then it was over, the pageant blacked out. We all felt the sting. Tony was a young colleague of ours, and we have been searching during these first days, for answers. Why?

Kathy (Tony's thirteen-year-old) and I were by the big pine south of this chapel yesterday. We met by chance, picking up the fallen cones. We spoke of her father. I told her about seeds, thousands of seeds that nature throws away before one catches a soil and springs up; how few reach the first stages of development; how precious and fragile is a single life; how nature's children are numberless and none entirely neglected, nevertheless there are favorites on whom much is squandered and for whom there are great sacrifices.

Thirty-seven years he stood in the rain and the sun. He was nourished and loved by a mother. He was a school boy with his satchel and shining morning face. He stood tall under the stars and to a green altar led her mother and passed the precious seed to Kathy. So now she stood under this green tree, this blue sky.

Tony left Gustavus a legacy. He was an able administrator. He loved his students and his discipline. He brought them together with hand-tailored programs. He had such dreams for the department and the college! Good students were coming. In the evening they went down to his house to talk.

For Tony, the issues were physics and something larger than physics, the mind awakened, understanding, metaphysics. The non-physics student should be taught physical concepts. All should become humane.

We are saddened to speak of these things as we realize the loss to our college and to ourselves. We must go now, returning Tony to the good earth of Michigan. Do not be afraid.

Julian (Tony) Crawford, Associate Professor and Chair of the Physics Department, joined the Gustavus Adolphus College faculty in 1967 and died April 17, 1969.

END OF THE VIETNAM WAR

April 30, 1975

He has frustrated the designs of the nations.

He defeats the plans of the peoples, his own design shall stand forever, the plans of his heart from age to age.

—Psalm 33:10

The war is over! Saigon has fallen to the communists. There is sadness, though not because we lost. For it to have ended this way was a victory of the spirit over the cynicism of naked force. We have said little about this war the last two years, because it didn't seem to be your war. You were not threatened by it. There was a time when the war was all we thought of, day and night. We are now hearing the speeches of our leaders Kissinger and Ford. I do not understand what they are saying. *All we are saying is give peace a chance.*

We are asked by President Ford to pull ourselves and our community together. We are asked to refrain from recriminating remarks about the sad events of last evening in Saigon. This is not easy. I cannot just forget! That is why I am here to pray today. We must forgive and be forgiven, but surely we must remember this war. Have we learned nothing? Are there not lessons we may take into our future, lessons essential to our being responsible for any future? We cannot just forget a decade of living, put it behind us as if it never happened, get on with the national basketball finals and the Emmy Awards.

It seems to me we need to take responsibility for what has happened. We must not allow this defeat to deprive us of our responsibility for history. It is not enough to maintain honor in the face of defeat, if we fail to face the future. The question is not how we extricated ourselves from this affair with dignity but how the coming generation is to live!

I thought the lesson we learned was not the one President Ford is selling, that we are the strongest nation on earth; that our enemies should be apprised that we will continue to honor all our commitments, no matter to whom or on what basis. Wasn't that the problem in the East—we didn't know for what or whom we were fighting? I thought we were beginning to think of ourselves as being one of the family with Britain and France, the northern countries. I thought we were ceasing to be the moralists of world, had no lessons to impart just now. I thought we were learning that deceptive and equivocal speech doesn't work. I thought we were learning that the administrative office should cease its suspicion of other branches of government and of the institutions in a democracy by which a free people expresses approval and dissent. I thought we were going to be more open and frank in our public discussion, instead of expressing this cynicism and these platitudes. I thought we intended to learn these lessons for our own common life on this little campus, in this state of Minnesota.

Will our spiritual reserves prove adequate to this hour? Can we be candid and remorseless about our failure to live up to our ideals? Could we be simple again and straightforward? These are ideals that are close to the heart of God, so he has frustrated the designs of the nations. I think that is what we are praying about today, to forgive, to be forgiven, surely, but more, to see more clearly. This prayer meeting we called is not for running away from our responsibility, for patching things over. It is for the courage to face it and the grace to go on! *Amen.*

MAY

JOSEPH NICOLAS NICOLLET

Grand age, nous venons de toutes rives de la terre. Notre race est antique, notre face est sans nom. Et le temps en sait long sur tous les hommes que nous fumes.

Nous avon marche seuls sur les routes lointaines; et les mers nous portaient qui nous furent etrangeres. Nous avons connu l'ombre et son spectre de jade. Nous avons vu le feu dont s'effaraient nos betes. Et le ciel tint courroux dans nos vases de fer.

Grand age, nous voici.

Great age, we come from all the shores of the earth. Our race is ancient, our face is nameless. And time has long known more than it tells of all the men we were.

We have walked the distant roads alone; and seas have borne us that to us were strangers. We have known the shade and his jade spectre. We have seen the fire that cast fear among our beasts. And heaven's wrath forked in our jars of iron.

Great age, behold us.

—Saint-John Perse

It is fitting that Joseph Nicolas Nicollet should return to stand upon the hill of this college, overlooking his lovely river valley, in a county which bears his name, Nicollet County, Minnesota. He fixed this land for all time upon the maps of the world. He would still teach us the science of the valley, its beauty and its divinity.

It is fitting that this Frenchman, exile, explorer, voyageur, whose last unaccomplished wish was to die in St. Peter territory, should return one hundred and fifty years after he first came to this valley, in the sculpted public art on a site in St. Peter. Nicollet, French explorer and scientist, was born in Savoie, France, in 1789. He died alone in a Washington, D.C., hotel room in 1843.

It is fitting that from where he stands, his gaze should be toward the river. One hundred and forty-eight years ago he came up that valley on horseback, zig-zagging his way, stopping at Traverse des Sioux, likely crossing the very land on which his image now stands, then to Oakleaf Lake over by my farm, on to Middle Lake and west to Swan Lake—all well known to you biology field majors. He came, drawing sketches of the land, how it lay, how the creeks and the streams and the rivers were interrelated, how the valley hills were thrown. We still treasure his maps. They are useful to this day!

In his notebooks, you may find the scientific names of the trees of the valley, and the shrubs, the flowers, the rocks, the soils, the animals! He was interested in everything in his surroundings, all manifestations of nature in fossils, in flora and fauna, in minerals and geological formations, in meteorological conditions. He stands as a witness to the liberal mind. Nicollet is a benchmark. You should measure yourself by him.

He measured the altitude of these hills by using barometers. At night, from them, he sighted the stars, the alpha star in Andromeda, the alpha star in Cygnus. He linked the land and the stars.

In our imagination we see him ambling up the valley on his horse with his baggage, instruments, pebbles, plants, birds, reptiles, quadrupeds, medicine bags, moccasins, peace pipes. We think him a fine fellow. We are glad to welcome him here. May generations yet to come to this college see him too, learn from him a love of the things of this valley, the things of this world, of things for their own sakes!

It is fitting that M. Nicollet should stand, placed in front of Jacob Uhler Hall, sextant in hand. Uhler was the great polymath of Gustavus. A mathematician and scientist, he once taught all of the sciences here, physics, chemistry and biology. In 1883 he founded the physics laboratory. Subsequently he also founded laboratories in chemistry and biology. He died in 1937 after fifty-five years as this college's most popular and influential teacher. Nicollet, as polymath, is even more astonishing!—astronomer, mathematician (friend of LaPlace), economist, barometrician, geographer, cartographer, anthropologist, ethnologist (the merit of his writings even now brought to light by Melva Lind's research), geologist, humanitarian, philosopher—a liberal mind indeed! It is fitting he should stand in the midst of this college of arts and sciences devoted to the liberal mind. It is fitting that this college should stand on Nicollet's land.

It is fitting that Nicollet should stand in a college that belongs to the church. He was a churchman, an intimate of bishops, a frequent guest at seminaries. He was very devout. His dear ''Providence'' he apprehended everywhere in the living geometry of rocks and crystals, in the design of flowers, in the weather, fair or foul; in the supplies of food and water; in the good will of Chippewa and Sisseton Sioux. This ''Providence'' tested him in reverse of fortune, loss of friends, in the sadness of life. For Nicollet God was everywhere, in the music of his violin, in the pauses between the notes. When the dining was done, when the evening came on, when the conversation paused, he picked up his violin. His friends said, ''He played like an angel.''

Last, it is fitting that Nicollet should stand in this college as a gift from one of its scholars, an administrator and most singular lady, Dean Melva Lind. After education at the Sorbonne and teaching at Mt. Holyoke, and deaning at Wellesley, she returned to her native land to be a professor and dean in this college. Over the years she has brought us news, news of other lands, faraway cities, continental cultures. News of Minnesota politics, of French *lettres*. Thanks to her, the eastern seaboard came closer. Europe came closer. Her Midwestern students learned not to fear society, or the intellect, or the humanitarian impulse of the well-placed. And they discovered what glitter there was in their own gifts for adventuring in that world. Then she taught them about Minnesota.

Nicollet, near death, fifty-four years of age, in Washington, D.C., far away from this valley, health ruined by many journeys, by anxieties, in his last letters wrote, "I dream of but one thing. That if you pass another winter at St. Peter's, I ask of you the hospitality of coming and finishing with you three volumes that I want to publish as soon as possible."

Nicollet! *O vous, homme de France!* O you, man of France, come and finish your work. We will help you!

SPRING SERMON

Ah Spring!

It marches on the valley for the ten-thousandth time since the glacier, saunters through the campus yards for its 102nd performance. Don't miss the show! Bird song in the campus mall Sunday mornings at seven. Lilac darkness when night comes on. Purple crocus on the chapel green, yellow-bellied sapsucker down in the Alexis birch, nights pricked with tiny tender stars, trees stir, south wind, O promise me. The forlorn night freight train in Kasota calls away. O far away from here where I am going. What will I be? What will I be?

Ah me! A sighing chaplain fancies banquets and booze in the woods. He will not now read all the books in Bernadotte, nor say all the prayers at Christ's. One last look at the body parade across the dear, dear space, full flesh, full flower now, a last unfolding before the world ends. Never leave me, never leave me. Will it ever end? Will it last the millennium?

I remember the revolution eight years ago, after the killings at Kent state. The Gusties figured it was the last spring, so they left school. This is what I said to the few who stopped by chapel on the way out:

The Revolution, you say! I will make it difficult for you before you go. Tomorrow you must choose how you will dispose of May. Your concern about this war is very large and fills the whole horizon. Many of you feel that school is beside the point. But you must not all think that way. Some of you should turn in and sleep for a while. Some of you should go back to the books you left when you ran out into the streets. You have not copped out if you study. If you leave, what will you have in two weeks? The planet will still be here. It will require then, as it does now, whatever courage you can bring to living. O be wise! Only this morning, when it was still dark, you lay over here in dormitory slumber. Out in the country, I heard a whippoorwill call from the deep woods along the river, as Spring advanced along the valley for the ten-thousandth time since the glacier. Be very wise.

ST. COPERNICUS

Eleven years ago in November, when my daughter was born, I wrote a poem in which I expressed the wish that the good God would let her dance through the autumn universe. Eleven autumns have passed since, and there has been dancing in a farm home of Minnesota, as homey as old Gospel hymns and tales of the brothers Grimm. The dear hunter Orion whom I invoked in the poem, has chased the great Bear across the night sky over the farm, again and again.

This year she has begun to imagine that there might be another way of seeing it. It was something the teacher said at public school. The stars in Orion are far apart. The hunter is your imagination. And the other day her little brother Geoffrey asked her what happens to the sun when it goes down behind Johnson's barn. Does it fall into a hole in the ground? So it was time for the story of Uncle Nicolas Copernicus.

He's the saint on today's church calendar, only I told the children to call him uncle. Makes them feel involved in what Uncle Nick might have done or said. Uncle Nick studied theology at the University of Cracow. He spent almost all his life as a cleric attached to the cathedral in the little town of Frombork on the Baltic Sea—the remotest corner of the Earth. When he wasn't saying Mass, he was doctor, lawyer, land manager for the bishop and his flock—often on horseback in mid-winter, in remote villages providing the peasants with livestock and seed, fixing rents, allocating relief. On one of these journeys, due to a local war, he was trapped in the castle at Olsztyn for a time. Fatigued by his excursions, weary of consultations, freed from the day-to-day hustle, he began work on an idea he'd considered for many years. The University had not only taught him how to play cards, drink beer and watch for the Vikings! The idea turned out to be quite revolutionary, as it will always be as long as this civilization lasts, as it will be for my daughter when with her new questions she carefully considers what Uncle Nick has to say: ''So many authorities say the earth rests at the center of the universe, that people think the contrary supposition ridiculous. If however we think about it, we will see that the question has not yet been decided, and is by no means to be scorned. For every apparent change in place occurs because either the thing seen moves or the seer moves. Now it is from earth that the stars are seen and presented to our sight. Therefore, if the earth moves, it will appear in the stars as the same movement, but in the opposite direction, as though the stars themselves were passing over. The nightly revolution of the stars is such a movement. If you admit that the heavens possess none of this movement, but that the earth turns from west to east, you will find that as regards the apparent rising and setting of the sun, moon, and stars, *this is the case!*''

There is a contemporary of Uncle Nick, who lived a hundred miles away from the town of Frombork, in a town named Wittenberg. He was also a cleric, a college professor attached to the castle church where occasionally he said Mass: Dr. Martin Luther. He also has his saint's day in the calendar. I tell the children to call him Uncle Marty. Like Uncle Nick

Copernicus and Cross

112

he was imprisoned by events in a castle with time on his hands. That was 1521, and the castle was the Wartburg. He used his time to translate the Bible into German, and with the translation to create a new language, a new era. Now, his book and Uncle Nick's book were subsequently published by the same person in Nuremberg. Still, he and Uncle Nick never met.

Each died in his little town—three years apart; Uncle Nick in 1543, Uncle Marty in 1546. Stranger than fiction, isn't it? Two clergy persons—stuck in small towns, saying Mass, reflective types though. Uncle Nick thinking about motion and the stars. Uncle Marty thinking about emotion and the Mass.

One evening after supper at the Luther house (beer and bratwurst), with his students gathered about, Uncle Marty said, "that fool Uncle Nick will overturn the whole system of astronomy." Now that is ironic! From the Uncle who would overturn the whole system of theology! Is there anyone, who after 500 years has not heard the one about the theologian who said heaven was not a place in the sky above the stars, but an attitude of the human heart? Luther did. He maintained that heaven was a symbol for God. Since God was everywhere present, heaven was everywhere present. Furthermore, since Christ ascended into heaven, he ascended to everywhere including the altars of the future Lutheran church. To quote Uncle Marty: "The right hand of God is not a place. It is God's omnipotent power, which is at the same time nowhere and everywhere. It is present at all places, even in the belly of a cockroach, even in the smallest leaf of a tree." Now that overturns a few ideas!

Dear children. It is five hundred years since Uncle Nick and Uncle Marty worked together, apart, in central Europe. Their awesome thoughts remain. The first thought is Uncle Nick's. That this chapel spire spins about the sun ninety-three million miles away. The second thought is Uncle Marty's: that at the altar beneath the spire which is nowhere in the universe, the God, the ground of Universal Being is present as bread.

SERMON FOR THE END OF A TERM

Summertime and the living is easy.
She comes, careless, indifferent
To our concerns. . .lazy afternoons,
Restless nights in high-powered cars,
South winds stirring the new leaves.
O Wind of spring, since I dare not know you
She threatens to undo all concern
For the duties of the academic life.
She arrives when we least need her.
She tempts us with her new green prints.
She sings in the grass.
She softens the brain.
Exasperating!
Other seasons of the year
Fit the college calendar.
Not so the first warm days before last examination.
Examination belongs to dark days of autumn rain,
To bracing days of January cold,
When the mind is sharp,
For fill in the blank, multiple choice,
Classify the bird.
Summer days are for truths more vague, less defined,
For old ideas, forsaken by philosophy.
But we may not determine the times.
So I call you to resist this summer temptress.
Go against her dictates!
Cram! Memorize! Keep from disintegrating before Tuesday.

Let me console you with a story.
It concerns a very demanding professor in this college,
A real straight! His brain has softened!
Two months ago he promised a comprehensive examination.
Last night he puttered in the back yard until after dark,
And spent the remainder of the evening in front of the telly.
On this Reading Day you are preparing for an exam
He has not yet written!

In a few days, many of us will be in that line
Of black-gowned clerks
That winds its way through the campus mall to the stadium.
It is always a lovely vision and a moving experience.
For those of us who walk behind,

You graduates are an answer to the question, what is the difference?
You embody the days of our years.
You take with you a part of our lives we have lived in
For a visionary moment; you are an ancient procession of pilgrims
Passing through a holy wayside,
A symbol of our human aspiration,
A symbol of divine grace.

PENTECOST: FESTIVAL OF THE HOLY SPIRIT

Here's to you, '82. In the name of the Father, and of the Son, and of the Holy Spirit.

On this last great day of the feast, not of the fools but of the wise, in this house of Christ on the great day of the Spirit—the same day in which you will become a bachelor of arts from this fair college—it is salutary for you to remember what it is that has brought you here: the Spirit of God. The Spirit of God who, wearing the bright fabric of nature, has held you fast in her rhythms night and day and change of season, *the force that through the green fuse drove the flower, drives your green age.* Once you were a sniveling freshman—as Shakespeare says, "mewling and puking"—a seedling, an unripe something that stood around in the mall centuries ago, checking into a room, sending Mom and Dad to the chapel to find what possible protection we could give you without them, kissing Mom good-bye and meeting the group leader, going to the square dance, the small group meetings, the dinner, the variety show, auditioning for the choir, wondering what your major was and how to change it, and repeating a hundred times that you were from a small town somewhere near Duluth. Something unripe was planted here, a tiny seedling, a few disorganized brain cells in an organism. But it was driven by the Spirit, summer and winter, springtime and harvest, atom and chlorophyll and star and oxygen—and in this garden it grew, early on experiencing the pain of the professor's pruning shear, whole branches cut off and thrown away, but something evolving in a strange and beautiful way, something by the seasons checked and then cheered—again in Shakespeare's words, "Hour by hour we write and write," until we came to the longest winter of all and the last spring, a certain richness now of branches, of flower, of fruit—we've come full cycle, first the blade, then the ear, and then the full grain. From that disorganized organism of cells, you have become this complexity of body and mind which we celebrate today and of which we are so proud. Something was planted and it grew, shaken by storms but enduring to this last spring, ripening mostly unseeing and unseen. But, brothers and sisters, you were carried! Praise to the Spirit.

So we are in this house of Christ on the great day of the feast of the Spirit. I hope that you will understand that not only nature, but history in the form of this college is a masque of the Spirit.

You are the twentieth class I have watched come this way and I have come to observe over the years that only as you near graduation, sometimes in these last weeks, do many of you learn what the real object of the college is. This may seem unfortunate (what were you doing here, Elijah?!) until I reflect that when you do finally know what it was, know for yourself and on your own terms all that preceded, that seemed so scattered—that recognition is not lost, but is caught up, is realized in the flowering of that recognition, so that you know something now at the end of college and will know it for the remainder of your life, the value of a certain kind of inquiry, an attitude of mind, a curiosity about life which will prevent you from becoming the most deadly sort of person—bored and boring—and the achievement of an intellectual sincerity, which will prevent you from becoming conventionalized in the wrong way, which would prevent you from ceasing to know yourself in every decade of your life. Still more, you have learned a discipline which will prevent the intellectual in you from degenerating into a curiosity of the merely pecking kind which never organizes anything, and which will add sincerity to humility, which will keep sincerity from degenerating into plain egoism.

Moreover, the object of the college is (was) to set before you the great world as a spirtual order—in it you were intended to live so that others would have confidence not only in your honesty but also in your wisdom and in your courage—to set before you the world as a moral world, held up by moral structures, in which to live is to transcend mere pleasure and ambition. It would surely grieve the Spirit of this college if you do not want to be better than others in the ethical world, if you dread being thought self-righteous, for it is a needless fear which always lowers the tone of any group to which you belong. Brothers and sisters, what you will actually find in the world, yes, even in the military and corporate structures (as a surprise to some of you) and sometimes not to be found in the church structure, are thousands of people who have not bowed the knee to Baal, people who live ethically and are not thought to be self-righteous. If you have any insight into the deeper springs of human nature, you will meet them constantly in your journey through life. If you have not, you will not see them, because they do not make a show of virtue, but they have it! They uphold it in others because they are there, by their example! And they make the world possible by their existence.

Now everything for which this college stands expects you to be numbered in its company— the Spirit in nature, the Spirit in the masque of the history of this college, and finally, that we are in this house of Christ on the great day of the Spirit because the Spirit of nature and the Spirit of history have come to us as the Spirit of Jesus Christ. We are participating this day in the living and unbroken experience of the body of Christ on this which may be the 1953rd Pentecost—Erling will have to correct me, or Clark, as to whether it's 52 or 54. But this body of Christ is still the sacrament of our world, the sacrament of the Christic dying and rising which we must all inevitably accomplish in our own bodies and for our own time. And so we take into our own hands the whole world as if it were a loaf of bread and a cup of wine, and we pledge ourselves to the continual transformation of its reality, the continual transformation in the Spirit.

We know this communion of the Spirit in the freedom in which we accept responsibility, where there is no apparent offer of success or advantage, where we accept the world's fragments of beauty and love purely, simply, as the promise of beauty and love without the cynicism which says this is a cheap form of consolation for some final deception, where we accept each day's existence from a presence, sometimes a very dark presence, sometimes light, but always mysterious and always resourceful so that we can go on and do what we must do, where we entrust all our knowledge and all the questions along the way to the silent and all-inclusive mystery which is loved more than all our individual and particular knowledge, which makes us such a small people. What a liberation this is for living, the Spirit communing with our spirit, slowly turning our cool knowledge into the raging hunger that accompanies our prolonged Pentecost. The promise to you is as old as Pentecost. "I will put my Spirit in you," said the prophet Ezekiel, "and you will live." And in the Acts: "I will pour out my Spirit upon you." And this promise is to you and to your children.

So it is, brothers and sisters, as we return from the light and joy of the Spirit's presence in Christ, we will always recover the world as a meaningful field of our action. Then we may understand the true reality in the world and thereby discover what we must be in the midst of that reality. This mission is always at its beginning. The Church is not any older than this hour. It is today that you are sent back into the world in joy and peace, having seen the true light, having partaken of the Holy Spirit, having been a witness to divine love.

These are high words. Let us not fool ourselves. I don't fool myself. We are all of us, even the most religious and holy, secular. We live in the world again and again (we may this afternoon) as if there were no God, but we may be saved from ourselves again and again. By the Spirit's grace we may live in the world, seeing it as a sign of God's presence, know the joy of his coming, the call again and again to community, the hope for an ultimate fulfillment. Since Pentecost there is a seal, a way, a sign of the Spirit, on everything for those who receive the life of the Spirit of Christ and know that it is the hidden life of the world, and that in that life lived for us and in us, the world in its totality becomes a liturgy, a communion, an ascension. *Amen.*

O God the Holy Ghost, come to us and among us. Come as the wind and cleanse us. Come as the fire and burn. Come as the dew and refresh. Convict and consecrate us to our great good and to your greater glory. In the name of Christ. Amen.

THE PRODIGAL SON

Today we hear the familiar story of the prodigal son, the father and the other brother: a poignant, winsome parable that always speaks to us. Jesus' critics didn't understand why he loved prodigals and disdained the conventional elder brothers, so he told the parable of the wastrel son who took his share of the family estate and wasted it in riotous living in the far country. How he ended up as a farm laborer, eating with the pigs, and of how he came to himself and went back home to confront his father. He said "Father, I have hit bottom. I am not worthy to carry your name. I would be willing to be one of the servants." Then Jesus told how the father, a stately gentleman who never ran from anything (rich so he didn't need to run), saw his son on the road, ran toward him, embraced him, kissed him, killed the fatted calf.

It's a wonderful story. I shall always want to hear it again. It is your story, you the children of gentry in America, children of opportunity and promise. You have taken your share of the family money, and have come down to college to prepare for a profession. But now after a year or two, it appears that you have wasted it! You haven't done much. There were so many distractions! Relationships! Time passed quickly and today you are sitting in this church all dressed up, among the husks. You say to yourself, "Why go on with this? I'll go home and say to the folks: 'Look folks, I am not worthy to go to college, to enter a profession; let me take a job at the plant sweeping floors. Perhaps I could go downtown to the Dairy Queen. I'm not worthy to be a child of this family. Just let me come home.' "

Having come to yourself, with the knowledge that you have hit bottom—willing to do anything, any work in this society—facing your father with it: a remarkable change takes place in the current reality of your miserable life, because you have come to yourself! You see that you must change your life. You saw all along that things were not going well, but you were not doing anything about it. Now you decided to do something, if only to admit that you are going nowhere.

"No," your father says, "if you have changed your mind, you are a true son of the family. You should go on preparing for something, so let's go to dinner."

This is a parable about two brothers. The elder brother is as fascinating a study in human character as the prodigal. He didn't break with the father's will. Receiving his portion of the family goods, he invested them well. He did the father's work. He came down to Gustavus and never broke the traces. All went well. If he attended the fraternity rush party, he didn't get drunk, didn't stay around with the pigs in the swill of the barn. His studies went well, his relationships in place. He made progress toward a profession. It is true that he took few risks. He played it safe, but there was peace with the folks. He was faithful to his prayers, he followed the commandments and the father was pleased. "Son," he says, "you've been a dear son. We've always been together on things. There hasn't been any separation, no alienation between us. Therefore, everything that is mine is yours."

What was wrong with him? Why is the elder brother unhappy and resentful? Why doesn't he adopt the father's gracious attitude toward the younger brother? Since everything has gone well with him why isn't he happy? Instead he is angry. He begrudges his brother this homecoming. What a wretched thing to be a Christian in the Father's house, but essentially a grumbling, unhappy person. Even in the midst of your obedience, your doing the right thing, you are feeding on the husks. You are not a real son.

The problem is your attitude, not your behavior. It is your attitude toward your situation, and toward your brothers and sisters. What is your attitude toward your brother? "Look, Dad, this so-called son of yours has squandered his money and our reputation. He has ruined his life, so he crawls home, and you give him another chance. I resent that."

When the feast begins, he refuses to sit at table with his brother. He wants to kick him back into the gutter somewhere. The father comes out of the house to reason with him. He says to the father, "That son of yours, the useless one, that womanizer, how could you kill the fatted calf for him? You've never done it for me and my friends." The father answered him, "That brother of yours—your brother—was lost, but now he is found, was dead but now is alive." The elder son said, "That son of yours." The father said, "That brother of yours!" Perhaps it was the reminder that did it! Your brother, your sister. Look around you, Gustie. See the person of whom you don't approve! Your brother. So they went into the feast together. Come to the table!

MELLOW 1975

Simply looking around the other day, standing in the late afternoon sun out at the barn—or was it yesterday in the dining common? Mom, will there be eggs on Monday?—looking for a last word to this class. For my effort among you, you gave me one, and it was the same word whether over beer or eggs by which you described yourself. . .mellow. The mellow class.

Something unripe stood around here four years ago checking into a room, sending Mom and Dad to the chapel with a campus map, to find out if you would be taken care of, in sickness and in health. That something unripe, ripened! Grew up, filled out, cheered and checked by the seasons—increased, came on, came painfully, leafing out, branched, flowered, fruited. Something was planted in those first days that grew, and though by storms shaken, remained through the long winter into the long afternoon, mellowed. That was you.

Your mellow may have been a reaction to the hyperactive, acidic predecessors of yours, the sixties students. Your mellow for us professors was a retreat, a respite, a return to the gardens of the fifties whence we came, a return to the ivory tower. How peaceful it became after a while. We were tired of the sixties. The college became itself again, away from the intrusive stimuli that interferred with growing. The cows returned to Cambridge fields, and it was forever. We played again, games for games' sake. There were three hots every day, a roof at night, clean sheets when you needed them, plenty to drink, the halls grew ivy. It was mellow.

We lost track of time. One looked over the hedge. There was a world of commerce out there, but it could wait—suburbs, government, church, business, summer houses, nothing worth pursuing now, let's stay here. Perhaps we needn't ever leave. What time is it? What summer is this? The resort is closing down? Pass the steak. Swish the wine in the glass. Savor it once more. This restaurant is closed? I can't come back next year? The room is reserved for someone with another name? It's someone else's turn? Stop pushing!

We aren't pushing. It's your little brothers and sisters! "Well now, we're sorry, but it's our turn to do this that you've been doing, so take your stuff and go wherever it is that you're going. There isn't room for everyone here in this garden."

So, you may not see anything out there that interests you, but you can't stay, because the rooms are rented to someone else, and you are too old for a reservation and your bill is already too large, and the games aren't that much fun and it's time to go. For God's sake, for society's sake, for self's sake, you'd best go. You can't prolong this afternoon of your life.

Take what you know, and go out there and create your own garden! Go to work. It's not so bad. Actually, it's more interesting than having nothing to do tomorrow except to get up for a late breakfast, watch a ball game, read a book, go to a party. It's all right to take care of yourself, with no one to fall back on. You might even become creative, find and create objects of real meaning and worth, something better than drugs and drink and ordinary sex, something better than the love of ideas alone, and the analysis of the parts of things, a life of accomplishment.

Good-bye, mellow. It was good. You can come back when you need to. We won't even remember how unmellow you were sometimes. We will always remember the youth and the life and the beauty and the goodness you brought here in your time. We thank you for that. The Lord be with you, mellow, as you go. The Lord be with you, mellow President and Mrs. Barth, Frank and Marge. Thanks for everything. Please, please always come back, you will always belong to us.

Frank R. Barth, tenth President of Gustavus Adolphus College, served from 1969 to 1975.

TELL THEM THAT THEY WERE GOOD

Class of 1980

For wisdom, the fashioner of all things, taught me. For in her there is a spirit that is intelligent, holy, unique, manifold, subtle, mobile, clear, unpolluted, distinct, invulnerable, loving the good, keen, irresistible, beneficent, humane, steadfast, sure, free from anxiety, all-powerful, overseeing all, and penetrating through all spirits that are intelligent and pure and most subtle.

—Wisdom of Solomon, 7:22-23

It is the privilege of this preacher to pronounce upon you people the benediction of this house of learning; as it will be the task of the Honorable Wendell Anderson this afternoon to address you upon the lessons for tomorrow (I expect he might suggest how to lose public office graciously); as it will be the charge of your classmate Eiden of Brainerd to salute the memory of your brief existence here. But mine the very best part, to say on behalf of my academic colleagues, good-bye girl, it was good, storm and laughter, even the wounds and hurt and bitter experience which have made us strong together, and sunk our roots deep in this Gustie experience. Only Thursday, on my way to the Barn, after declining to come along, Hamrum shouted after me, "Padre, tell them that they were good."

So good-bye! You understand it's important we say good-bye to you, otherwise you might not know that you have been here. And because we must say good-bye before we can say hello again. Some of you wanted to go already last November. You don't mind our saying good-bye. It took so long to get around to it! Others of you don't understand yet—that is, you have to go! You have to go so that you can come back. It's all right to go, you know!

Today we bid farewell to a great skipper and his family, captain of His Majesty's ship Gustav Adolph for five years. My captain! When you came aboard we were floundering in troubled waters. You unfurled our mainsail and we caught the wind again, and we sailed! We ran before the wind, swiftly, swiftly. You drove us hard. We were strong again because you were strong. It is not an easy craft to steer, but you brought us to a port, from which we might put out again, bilge free. Thank you, sir; this voyage will never be forgotten. Godspeed, Edward Lindell, Patty, Paul, Eric.

Today we need to number our days that we may get a heart of wisdom. We need some sense of the constant and the kind, in the inconstant dark. This wisdom in our text refers to the dynamic constants that surround us, the knowledge of which leads to an artful way of living and a relationship to God. There is a dynamic divine order inside things, a deep structure, like Platonic ideas and Aristotelian forms, and Thomistic laws and Leibnizian monads, and Kantian categories, and Bonhoefferian mandates. "Two things fill the mind with ever new and increasing admiration and awe, the oftener and more steadily they are reflected on, the starry heavens above me, and the moral law within me." So Kant at the conclusion of his mighty *Critique of Pure Reason*. This symmetry is the creative ordering of God, and its manifestation along our thinking path is called by these ancient writers, the wisdom of God.

This wisdom is a treasure, and we should seek her. She is the structure of the world and the activity of the elements. She is the beginning and end and middle of times. She is the cycle of the years and the constellations of the stars. She is the natures of animals and the tempers of wild beasts. She is the powers of spirits and the reasonings of men. She is the varieties of plants and the virtues of roots. She is more mobile than any motion. She penetrates all things. She is more beautiful than the sun and God loves nothing so much as the person who lives with wisdom.

Ask the wild beast and he will teach you, and the birds of the air, they will show you, and the plants of the earth they will tell you, and the fish of the sea, they will teach you. Ask the day that uttereth speech and the night that sheweth knowledge. And we may elicit its crystalline structure with our mathematics and grasp its cycles in the migratory habits of birds, and cube its forms with paints on canvas, compose its harmonies, even as solitary Bruckner composed the Mass we offer on this day.

Moreover, this wisdom, this divine order is the dynamic within our common life. It is the dimension of our power to endure amidst chaos, to accept the difficult with a view to resolution. Each of us learns sooner or later, that there is in our common life a constancy and resource, a deep structure upon which we may call when the sunshine and prosperity, health and success of our surface life is not equal to the disappointments that always appear on that same surface. In some of our best moments we even welcome the adversity in order to test the reserve. You will come to know this in life, Gusties. Baker, there are still more difficult pitches to be thrown! Schoenebeck, you have only begun to turn upfield into the crunch! Erickson, there are more difficult challenges ahead than playing Chopin and translating Camus. But there is in all of you a deep structure, steadfast loyalties, a power to labor and endure, a higher power upon which you may throw yourself when your human strength gives out. This is the wisdom of God.

This deep structure is not only personal, it is social, the deep and abused foundation upon which any society is formed, the wisdom by which this spring the fields were planted; the wisdom by which the daily business of our town proceeds; the wisdom by which a nation lasts for two hundred years; the wisdom by which we challenge the yet unknown.

O good-bye, I know you must go. There is a word alongside Kant and the ancients, a glad word which brings us together this day. *The Wisdom from on high has visited us to guide our feet into the way of peace!* There is a wisdom that does not demand, it gives, because you are weak and selfish, and deaf and blind to the demands of the deep structure. There is a second wisdom which comes to restore the first as a human possibility. The meaning of the Christ-presence is herein contained, that God comes to us as love and healing after we have broken ourselves upon life's demands. He sends us out to meet them again. You come back broken from the field, he sends you out again. You lie and steal and cheat. You live in untruth and hypocrisy. He forgives and sends you back to rebuild what is broken. The fellowship of Christ, and the bread and wine we share in it this morning are the pledge of that restorative Wisdom in our midst.

With praise and thanksgiving, to God everliving, the tasks of our everyday life we will face.

Edward A. Lindell, eleventh President of Gustavus Adolphus College, served from 1975 to 1980.

JUNE

TRINITY SUNDAY

1983

Today we think about three personal manifestations of one God: God the father, mother, creator; the same God, Jesus Christ brother, sister, redeemer; the same God, Holy Spirit, son, daughter, sustainer; holy many, holy trinity, one God. I hear a low Gustie groan! Uff! that's heavy stuff, and you won't even have to answer for it, Elvee, off on sabbatical next year, so you leave us your foul theology on this fair day of our graduation. In any event, we wished to hear about ourselves! How we walked through the dappled sunlight of the Gustie years.

Checkmate! When I talk about God, I talk about you. I talk about the world, your world, the world that is coming toward you. That world without God is not the world, so we must talk of God and of you, because God without you is not God.

"O.K. Elvee, you're in the box, so what is happening in the world?"

First, you are graduating today from a "Swedish" college located in Minnesota whether you like it or not. For my own part, I don't always appreciate it. The Swedes imagine that this moveable feast is spread entirely with their dishes, that this was a Swedish accomplishment and I don't think they have been able to do this without us Swede-Hollanders, Swede-Irish, Swede-Jews, even without us Swede-Norwegians! We who gather in this room to graduate know who is the cement, do we not? Grandmother, you know the ethnic genes in your graduating grandson aren't all Swede.

But let us give them their due. Particularly on this Trinity Sunday. We have learned something from them. And they have instructed us in a few important matters beside meatballs and folk dancing and how not to tell a joke. No one has taught us more than the Swedes about the meaning of the first article of the creed, of God as creator. From Edgar Carlson and John Kendall, from Erling and Esbjornson and Johnson we have learned what it could mean to be able to say, "I believe in God the Father Almighty, Creator of Heaven and Earth." Because of them we are creationists, not narrow, reductionist, scientific creationists, but broad, compassionate, aesthetic creationists! They have taught us that faith embraces all of nature and history. They have taught us that God is at work in the birth and death of every organism in the great sensate web of life. They have taught us that God is at work in every human society, Christian, Buddhist, Muslim or secular, and that it is the same God whom we adore in hymn and sacrament on this morning. They have taught us that the world is gift and is sustained as gift even if the recipient does not recognize the grantor.

Could you for a moment sense within the eternal Now of being in this room that you are placed in this hour as a divine gift? Clearly you could describe everything in this room, even invisible things! Give us a detailed, scientific analysis that would surprise your relatives, astonish your parents, shock your professors...the molecular structures in the wood of the pews, with so much space between electrons you should be falling to the floor; the complex cellular tissues in all the livers in this room; the family and social distinctions that determine most of the attitudes toward this sermon. But the whole of it as your world—as it confronts you as the Now of your existence—can you say why it is, and why you should be in it, and why you should be responsible for it, and what your attitude should be toward it? The Swedes say it is gift, it is God, and it calls forth from us prayer and praise, gratitude and care. You say, "life is not God, life is hell," and the Psalmist says, "if I descend into hell, you are there." A good Swedish professor from Lund taught us this prayer: *"O God, my life is a little ripple on a sea of centuries. After a few years, no one will recognize my name. And yet you surround me on all sides. Wherever I turn, I meet you as if mine were the only journey through the skies, through the sea, through the earth. Give me that confidence in you which enables me to find meaning in the transient and humble details of my life."*

II

Second, what do we mean by God manifested in the Son, Jesus Christ? We mean that God, who upholds all times and all spaces, is focused in a time and space, in human form. The general God becomes a particular person, in order to become every person. Everything, everywhere, the great Object becomes a particular Subject looking out upon the great Object. That Subject is Jesus of Nazareth, who in the Spirit becomes the Christ in whose body we all share; becomes the representative person, who dies and all die in him; who lives and all live in him. Jesus the Christ is the universal person, the final person, the person who is everyone. If we view the Incarnation as a temporary visitation of a god from heaven for thirty-three years, this is not good enough. And if Christ leaves time with the historic Jesus and does not remain as the foundation of human life, *"the light that lights everyone who is coming into the world,"* it is not good enough. It banishes God to other realms of being than those from which we have our daily lives. It disincarnates him. And in each century after the first, he is diminished rather than increased. Our understanding is that he increases, that the Christ event is not over, that his suffering must be filled up with our suffering, that in us he suffers to the end of the world, so that when we baptize you into his body we pray that you will share the fellowship of his suffering!

Jesus is unique. There is no other foundation. Like God, he cannot be replaced, but also like God, he must be re-presented in all human life. Just as Christ re-presents God, so Christ is re-presented in the disciples who act in his name, or in his nameless brothers and sisters everywhere. There is a compelling story told by Jorge Luis Borges, of a god who was shattered and broken, so that his image was lost to humanity, so that his face became irretrievable. A Jew, Paul, glimpsed that face on the Damascus road when the light struck him down. A young Greek, John, saw it on Patmos Island in the full strength of the Mediterranean sun and sea. A Spanish lady, Teresa, saw it in the fading light of the late afternoon, but could not tell us the color of the eyes. A pilgrim from the low countries seeing it in Veronica's handkerchief in Rome, murmured, *"Lord Jesus my God, true God, is this then what your face was like?"*

Like the persons in Borges' story, I have also seen this face. I saw it on a street in Philadelphia in a Jewish face. I saw it in the face of a young girl just fallen on her roller skates, wondering whether to cry. I saw it in the aging face in my mirror this morning. *"O God, you hold the world in your hand. A thousand spaces are as a single space, a thousand faces as a single face. Your human self who struggled here on earth is not generations removed from us, but as close as the faces of others. Our fields are warm from his body. His tears still fall on the earth."*

III

The third manifestation of God is in the Spirit. Because all of the faces are not reconciled with all of the bodies; because all of the subjects are not reconciled with all of the objects; because all of the minds are not reconciled with all of the forces, the Spirit of God is the continuing promise in life that it shall be reconciled. *"When the Spirit of truth is come he will guide you into all truth."* It all began in one second story room in Jerusalem with a few Jewish faces. The Spirit of truth drove them out, scattered them all over the Greek faces in Antioch and Alexandria. Next were the Roman faces, at first the faces of slaves, at the end the face of the Emperor, then the faces of Byzantium, of France, of Germany, of Britain, Africa, the East, the secular faces in a modern city. There are no limits to the Spirit. The definitions keep changing. You can be a Jewish Christian, or a Greek Christian, a male Christian or a female Christian, a religious Christian or a secular Christian, a Buddhist Christian or a Hindu Christian. The One becomes so many. The many are One. The Spirit unites them.

A last word. You must now explore what it is the Spirit will do with your face along the highways of the world. We have shown you during these years some of the possibilities, and we have travelled some of the world's roads. Other roads, we have only dreamt of. You will travel them. We pray that along these roads you will become whole, that you will discover what it is to become saved together with the life of the world on these roads. This life must become for you a sign of God's presence, the joy of God's coming, the call to communion with God. There is a seal on these journeys. There is a sign of the Spirit on everything, for those who are in Christ, and know that his is the hidden life of the world, so that in his Spirit the world in its totality becomes a liturgy and a communion. *"Give me back, O God, by your spirit, the freedom to choose anew and go far in my ministry of reconciliation, and create something whole and good out of me before death comes. Amen."*

Edgar M. Carlson, ninth President of Gustavus Adolphus College, served from 1944 to 1968.

John S. Kendall, twelfth and current President, began his term in 1981.

131

SONATA BACCALAUREUS

Class of '85, Garry Trudeau, Doonesbury, Class of '68, has been dunning you in the press for weeks, demanding that you account for your four years. He addressed you two weeks ago in the Sunday comics:

> Members of the Class of '85, you have spent the last four years in a trance. Taking your cue from the highest office in the land, you have somnambulated unfeelingly through a wounded world, pausing only to debate the central issue of your era—student parking. Paradoxes abound. By accepting unquestioningly all you have been taught, you have learned nothing of value. As you have enriched your prospects, you have impoverished your souls. Perhaps these are your failings. Perhaps they are ours. Regardless, we bid you adieu with sorrow and regret. When I snap my fingers you will awake. You will recall nothing except sweet gauzy scenes of unspent youth.

There is some truth to that acute account of your existence, and don't miss it, even if it hurts. For the most part, however, it represents the envy of the classes of the '60s for every generation succeeding theirs who actually managed to enjoy their college years, and it is in celebration of yours that I have composed a little graduation sonata built around three texts.

FIRST MOVEMENT. *Superbamente.* Triumphantly. On a text from 1 Samuel 4:7, *"When the ark of the covenant reached the camp, all Israel raised a mighty shout till the earth resounded, and when the Philistines heard the noise of the shout, they said, 'What does this great shouting in the camp of the Hebrews mean?'"*

Today there is a shout from the camp of the Gusties, and we know what it means—that you welcome this day with a sense of triumph. All the requirements, deans, professors, Philistines, impediments, obstacles have been faced and overcome and you have raised a milestone on the journey of your life, of which there are, after all, not so many, as the Fifty Year Class present this morning will tell you. So this should be a triumphant day in your life. Touch it, taste its sweetness.

Moreover, this graduation is an occasion of joy and, beyond that, of astonishment to some of us at some of you, that the frail fumbling freshmen of a few short years ago could actually take the rudder of their college years in hand and steer it on through.

Finally, I remind you to enrich your triumphant *cantus firmus* with a whole symphony of gratitude, for you have been blessed, pushed along by the gentle forces of genes and seasons and angel voices. The beauties and joys of life have swept over you; people have been generous to you. It is not given to everyone to receive this much benefit. It is given to some, denied to others. So, as you rejoice today that you have reached this goal, you should at

Sonata Baccalaureus

the same time be grateful that the will of the universe, the will of life, the will of God has brought you hither, so that while you take responsibility for the victory, you must simultaneously say, *"Now thank we all our God, who from our mother's arms hath blessed us on our way with countless gifts of love."*

SECOND MOVEMENT. *Adagio.* To a text from Acts 21:5, *"Kneeling down on the beach we prayed and said good-bye to one another; we wept, we kissed, we were sad."*

Adagio. A song of parting, June's immemorial hymn to youth, the bridal wreath, the graduate's gown, the roadside roses, the sweetness of the campus yards, disturbing the curtains of our senses, elegance along the walks, against the wall, sad song, slow dance.

Only last September it was, that you said, "One more time around, around once more." But it was a whole, long year, so out to the Barn for Eppie communion, and a year full of sweet gauzy scenes of unspent youth. Oh, there was an occasional nightmare along the way, one horrible dream in which Wick said you were a credit short, sorry about that. "But," you said, "the folks are coming, they're expecting . . ." and then you woke up and it was Sunday and you were still a credit short, but suddenly, now, it is done, done it is. Did it take place, somewhere else, inside the dorm, the head, what, what happened, anyone know what I majored in? Well, so here it is. "Hurrah and good luck," you say, even to someone you didn't know. "Good-bye. Sorry we didn't have time to fall in love, but there are letters to write, applications to grad school to fill out, invitations to weddings, the student loan down at the bank. Oh, my God, what's it like out there, I mean, not coming back in the fall? Hello, Gustie, how're you feeling? Not too good, and you? Don't know. Let's go to the Nic. Nah, it's all so stale, and nobody's there." And already the dandelions have whitened three times, the lilacs last in the dooryard bloomed, sad song, slow dance, *adagio.*

THIRD MOVEMENT. *Andante Moderato.* Walking. To a combined text from Isaiah 40 and Romans 12, *"They who wait for the Lord shall renew their strength, they shall mount up with wings like eagles, they shall run and not be weary, they shall walk and not faint. . . . I beseech you, therefore, brothers and sisters, by God's mercy, that you present your bodies as a living sacrifice, holy, acceptable unto God, which is your intelligent service."*

Yesterday at a presentation of the new curriculum to the old grads over in Nobel, one of them cleared his voice and spoke up to complain that we have not taught you enough Bible these years, so that you were arriving at the seminaries of the Church spiritually unlettered. I was thinking about that in the early hours of this morning as I wrote this homily. His judgment likely stands up. Your predecessors were better versed in the Bible, perhaps even lived a more biblical life than you will, and most of you are not matriculating at the seminary, and that is all right with us. It was not our intention that you go to the seminary, but that you go out into all the professions and jobs of the workaday world. We are disappointed that you don't know the Bible better, but I think we would be more disappointed if you did not understand that this work in which you are about to engage is holy, is acceptable, is the reasonable will of God. That's what Gustavus is about now; actually, that's what it has always been about.

As apologetic as you may feel about what you're intending to do, as distant as you may feel from being engaged in anything of particular service to God, you are nonetheless called to just that—doing and serving. In whatever you do, there is a divine dignity to all work so long as one does it with humble excellence, and I think we will have failed you if you have missed this sense of "calling," of "vocation." We insist on a religious reading of our common life. We bear witness against the despair of those who think society isn't worth it. We bear witness against the deceptions of bureaucrats, the disillusionment of intellectuals. We bear witness that work is good and full of purpose, that your being here means something, that through the defeats and seeming futility of leading professional lives in America, a power far greater than your own is making for good on this earth, that in a world where we have suddenly begun to think of human life as cheap, the human community is still the one inconceivably precious thing with its dreams and its vision and its destiny. And membership in and service to that community is the highest and holiest of callings.

Now, it may be that this spiritual vision has not as yet become a part of your notion of success in your future profession. You have seen the pictures of success in *Forbes* and in *Fortune,* of someone sitting behind a mahogany desk gazing into the face of a computer. You have heard the echoes of this quantitative success, this struggle after money and power, in the advice given to you by your parents, in the corridors of this college by your professors. You have heard the gospel of success from the pulpits of the churches. But not from this church, not from these parents, not from our professors. We have suggested another dream for you, until here today and yonder you get on your feet and fashion some justice out of the facts of social life, some goodness that the Christ-spirit has let wistfully into your life. For we believe that back of our social agencies and those who contribute to them, back of the forces working for world peace, for the care of the sick and the relief of the poor, back of the steady drive for integrity in government and industry is that Christ-spirit, scattering about the daily life of us all such freedom, such camaraderie, such tenderness as we have.

Now, if some of you haven't heard many words in this room these last four years, if some of you have just today found it for the first time, hear me now. Gustavus, your college, will not measure your future success except by the service you give to the life of this world, human life, and all kinds of life.

So, we bid you good-bye. Many centuries ago in Greece at the origins of our civilization, the philosopher Plato stated that all good was God. I would echo that this morning. We bid you good-bye. We bid you God-bye. Have a good day. Have a God day. Have a good life. Have a God life. Serve the good. Serve God. We love you. *Amen.*

SUMMER ALTAR

In the winter laboratory,
I watched life disperse itself,
Into cells and chromosomes with their intricate chemical tracks;
Scatter itself abroad in a million integers,
Across minute multiple universes.
At the summer altar,
I watched all of it occur,
Once more,
As it were,
Fused together
And bound by love
In a single text.

Dear friends,
You have come here at the evening hour,
To be united as husband and wife.
It is a lovely day!
The gold of the roadside flowers
Has come into the church with you,
Where it glows in your garments and your faces.
These steps you took down this church aisle
To this altar,
Were the last in a long journey of life,
Which made possible your being here,
As they are the first in a life
To which you will make a larger contribution
Than you have made thus far.
It would be good that in this hour
You should remember the life that brought you here.
Once you were microscopic seeds in the universe,
Single cells. Life sustained and held you fast in her rhythms,
Faithfully carried you through embryonic centuries,
Through nights and days and change of season,
Atom, and chlorophyll, star, oxygen and love
Swept your destinies to this place.
The soft winds of summer fields,
The harsh storms of Minnesota,
Carried you to this complexity of body and mind.
You now before this altar make promises to that life.
Once too, you were sniveling children,

Sweet and sour.
We can hear the lost voices of your childhood.
We can see the land of your birth,
Where a parent and a grandparent generation secured for you shelters
Against the storms;
Where the ingredients of the good life were made your own,
Happy and sad experiences, easy and difficult times,
Against this time when you make your own way
After the manner of your own understanding.
You should be grateful,
Even for the storms which have made you stronger,
All your experience from birth till now,
All the love that nourished you at other times—
It is here with you as you continue the journey.

Parents!
You should also pause at the marriage of your children
On this late Saturday
In the summer of your lives.
Look about you in this church to see
Your parents, your children.
In a changing world, something has held,
Not unchanged, but holding, continuing:
A way of life, work, family, church,
The dignity of the person,
Competence, professionalism,
Personal fulfillment,
Service to society.
These values were a gift to you,
And you have passed them on.
Not unchanged! The family changes,
Yet the values remain.
If there is a beautiful vision in our century,
The restless twentieth century,
A vision of the earth being the Lord's,
This touches on it!
If there is a kingdom of which we are all members,
And for which we pray,
This touches on it!

Finally, dear children,
However many difficulties there are with marriage,
However many crosses are laid upon it,

Summer's Evening

138

It is a good thing you do here tonight.
We are happy for you, and hope,
That as you take on its responsibilities,
Of the care and nurture of one another,
In good times and in bad,
You will also come to know the rewards of marriage:
The sense of being linked in the generations of people
Who must go on in the earth, caring for one another;
So that each of you may be more fulfilled together
Than could have been possible as separate individuals;
That your common life in turn will be for the good of life around you.
Peace. *Amen.*